She Will Never...

Best wishes

Amanda Adams

7/10/22

She Will Never...

Achieving my Vision with a Visual Impairment

Publications

Amanda Harris

Published: September 2022 Ladey Adey Publications, Ancaster, Lincolnshire UK.

Amanda Harris has asserted her right to be identified as the author of this Work in accordance with the Copyright, Designs and Patents Act 1988.

ISBN: 978-1-913579-47-0 (Paperback).

ISBN: 978-1-913579-48-7 (e-publication).

British Library Cataloguing-in-Publication Data.
A catalogue record for this book is available from The British Library.

Cover Design by Abbirose Adey, of Ladey Adey Publications.

Cartoons by Chris Ryder, Witty Pics Ltd.

Author Back Cover Photo : Gemma Wilks, Stand Out Get Noticed Ltd.

Dedication

For Mum and Dad, Martyn and Matthew

Once we accept our limits, we go beyond them.
Albert Einstein

Contents

She Will Never...

Vivien Jones

Preface
Vivien Jones

My husband and I sat in complete bewilderment. What on earth was nystagmus?

"Nystagmus", **said the consultant,** *"Your baby son has nystagmus."*

Very little information was forthcoming, other than the statement that our son - then three months old - had *'a fifty per cent chance of normal school'* because of his visual impairment. It took me a long time to discover that this was a meaningless statement - by the time Sam was born (in 1983) most children with nystagmus went to mainstream school.

Because this was 1983, there was no easy way of accessing information. No internet, no way of reaching out to others who might have the condition. How I wish someone could have placed a copy of Amanda Harris' book *"She will never…"* in my hand all those years ago giving me a candid and illuminating account of growing up with a visual impairment. As it was, we fell into a kind of black hole of distress and lack of hard facts.

We did our best by quizzing our GP. I also rang a few organisations.

Through the research I was able to do, I established that nystagmus is a complex eye condition, characterised by involuntary movements of the eyes. They appear to wobble or flicker from side to side, up and down or round and round. At least 1 in 1,000 babies are born with congenital nystagmus. Many more people will acquire nystagmus later in life. There are currently few treatment options available, but researchers continue to work towards a better understanding of the condition, prevention and, eventually, a cure.

As I sought information, I happened to see a small article in a national newspaper stating that the London Refraction Hospital, now the Institute of Optometry, was conducting research into nystagmus. We took Sam to meet one of their leading practitioners at the time, Ron Mallett.

Mr Mallett was an encouraging and kindly man and we fell to discussing the difficulty for patients and their families of obtaining information about nystagmus. I was desperate to meet others with the condition who could perhaps answer my questions:

What could they see?

What problems did they encounter in education or at work?

We agreed that setting up a group for people living with nystagmus was a good idea. With Mr Mallett's help (remember this pre-dates data protection legislation!), I contacted other patients and most replied saying they would welcome the formation of a group. The first meeting took place at the end of 1984. I vividly remember one lady saying she didn't want the group to be for moaning about the condition - people wanted to exchange information and learn from each other, but hopefully in a positive way.

So, the Nystagmus Action Group was born. Subsequently, we changed the name to the Nystagmus Network® which seemed to better express what we were about. Largely through media coverage, we soon attracted attention from families who were as bewildered and distressed by the diagnosis and lack of support as I had been and from those with the condition who felt their needs had always been ignored. Answering their letters became the central focus. There was a huge unmet need for support. We also started to produce leaflets. Our graphics were fairly rudimentary, but people lapped up the information.

We began to organise events, too. Nothing beats human contact. Getting together with others at *'Open Day'* is the best tonic possible, in my view, for all of us living with nystagmus.

Computers and the internet changed everything, of course, allowing us to establish much more effective, and more attractive, communications. That said, talking to people going through diagnosis, or wanting advice, or just to talk about the condition is something we have always held dear. I am very glad we maintain this service in the charity today.

We became a registered charity in 1990 and appointed our first paid employee in 1997. New publications and a website followed. We also developed excellent relationships with researchers and clinicians. The action group I founded nearly 40 years ago continues to go from strength to strength. Social media has changed how we work - we are in touch with thousands of individuals and families as a result of it.

I am passionate about the positive role self-help groups like the Nystagmus Network can play in helping people. I remain frustrated that nystagmus is still seen as an obscure condition - at more than 1 per 1000 it is in fact relatively common and ought to be better known. I am proud of the role the Nystagmus Network has played over the years in supporting those with nystagmus - and conscious that there is still much, much more to do and many more people to reach.

Amanda Harris' book marks another breakthrough in terms of promoting knowledge about nystagmus. Amanda tells us that she has nystagmus with an underlying condition - as many do who have nystagmus. In her case, it is incomplete development of her optic nerves. I'm sure adults and young people who have nystagmus who read her story will share lots of her experiences and reflections. I hope, like Amanda, they will come to live with their nystagmus and even see the funny side on occasion. Anyone who does not have nystagmus themselves will come away from the book with a much better understanding of the condition and how it impacts the sight and life in general.

One of our current Nystagmus Network staff members, *Sue Ricketts*, has been privileged to read and comment on the first drafts of Amanda's book. She says,

> *"Your style is so lovely and engaging. I know people will enjoy reading your story, as I have done. It must be so difficult to stand back from your own experiences and read them as others might do,*

but you have hit exactly the right note in terms of: sharing, your open, approachable style and yes, your skill in making people want to read on! I had intended just to dip into the first couple of chapters and ended up reading right to the end!"

I entirely agree with Sue's comments. This is a book which will warm your heart and provide a lasting (and positive) insight into living with a visual impairment. So, thank you Amanda for helping to raise awareness of nystagmus by sharing your personal nystagmus story.

We are pleased to help promote the book and are grateful to Amanda for kindly donating a percentage of profits from the sale of the book in our online shop to the Nystagmus Network.

We wish Amanda every success with her first book and look forward to working with her in the future.

**Vivien Jones, Founder and Honorary President
The Nystagmus Network®**

She Will Never...

Andy Bounds

Foreword
Andy Bounds

Self-development books are funny things... Some contain lots of stories and experiences. They're engaging reads. But they can feel too much like the author's personal story. They're hard to take life lessons from. After all, the author's life is different to ours!

Whereas other books can be more the other way - lots of practical tips, but without the emotional pull.

But Amanda has managed to create a book that nails both! I emotionally connected with everything she has written. But, equally importantly, I now have lots of new techniques I can use after reading it.

The thing which hit me (and kept hitting me) is that our lives are basically shaped by:

What we do.

What is forced on us, whether we choose it or not.

How we react to both.

Although you may not have Amanda's visual impairment (an example of point 2 above), you'll have your own stuff that impacts you. Much of which you wouldn't choose. How successfully you react to these will play a huge role in how successful your life will be.

Amanda's story resonated with me on a personal level. Like her, poor eyesight runs in my family. My mum is totally blind. I'm blind in the left eye. My *'good'* eye has a prescription of -14.5 (anything under 10 is considered very short-sighted).

And, like Amanda, my poor eyesight has given me some challenges. I can't drive. I often bump into things on my left side. I can't even watch 3D films at the cinema (I have to buy those stupid 3D glasses - just so I can see things unblurred in 2D!)

And, again like Amanda, my visual impairment has given me wonderful blessings which probably wouldn't have happened without it.

For example, from the earliest age, I've been practising how to communicate from someone else's viewpoint. This has given me unusual skills and insight which directly led to me creating my award-winning Sales Consultancy business, writing best-selling books, and working all over the globe with some of the world's largest and most famous companies.

And even not driving has its benefits. Of course, there are times it's inconvenient - especially when the children were small, and I had to cart all their stuff around on public transport. But it's kept me healthier - I've walked at least ten miles per week since my teens. My children walk more than they would do if I could drive - it's all good.

So yes, we all have our things to deal with.

And so do others around us.

The better we're able to react to ours - and help them react to theirs - the more fulfilling our (and their) lives will be.

I'm excited for you (and for them) to read Amanda's techniques.

And I'm grateful to her for sharing with us, in such an honest, insightful and actionable way, these simple ways to improve all our lives.

Andy Bounds

Award-winning Sales Consultant and Best-Selling Author: The Snowball Effect and The Jelly Effect

www.andyboundsonline.com

She Will Never...

Amanda Harris

Introduction

Life isn't finding shelter in the storm.
It's about learning to dance in the rain.
Sherrilyn Kenyon

As a disabled person, I have had to learn to ask for help when I need it. However, my passion in life is to help others. Once people are aware of my disability, they rarely ask me for help. Throughout this book I will demonstrate how my experience may be able to help you to face your own challenges, or to help your friends and family to face theirs. Using my HR experience, I will also give some information about supporting disabled colleagues in the workplace.

This is my story and can be read as pure autobiography. It may make you laugh or cry in places. It includes information which can be used by organisations, businesspeople and individuals to give practical tips and details of organisations who can provide equipment and financial support.

I am visually impaired.

Please re-read the above statement. You are human, so it is likely that you will now be making some assumptions about me based on your knowledge and experience of visual impairment. That is fine - it is what we do naturally, and I won't be offended. By reading this book I trust you will gain some insight into my unique view of the world and what it is like to be different from others.

As with any ability or disability, my experience is unique, but I share some attributes, observations and frustrations with others who have a similar visual impairment to myself.

What is visual impairment?

Visual impairment is defined by the World Health Organisation as *'a decreased ability to see to a degree that causes problems not fixable by usual means, such as glasses'*. So, from birth my sight was assessed in relation to that of a *'fully sighted person'*. If everyone in the world had the same level of sight as me, then I would not have a disability. Society would have been constructed to meet my needs and those of the majority in society - just a thought!

Throughout my life, I have been told *"You will never..."* or, *"You should never..."* This is said by people who care about me and want to protect me.

But only I can see through my eyes! I am the expert on my limitations and aspirations. I know more about my eyesight than eye consultants, those who work with visual impairment, and my friends and family, because I live with it every minute of every day. This applies to you too, with whatever challenges you face, and whatever anyone says to you about them.

If I had believed everything I was told, I would never have done any of the amazing, frustrating or downright stupid things which have added so much colour to my life.

I have not always been labelled as visually impaired. At birth I was half blind, and I became partially sighted in my teens. I have been visually impaired for around twenty years now. Yet my sight has never changed. Whichever label is currently politically correct tells you nothing about the quality of my sight. I will never be offended by language.

Mine is an invisible disability. While researching this book I have asked family and friends to tell me how noticeable they find my visual impairment. They all said the same thing - sometimes my eyes wobble and I often use both reading glasses and a magnifying glass together to see better. But usually, my disability is invisible to others. Having an invisible disability can be a double-edged sword. I can choose to hide it, and my friends can forget about it and treat me as if I am fully sighted. However, the onus is then on me to ask for help when I need it. It is my responsibility (not theirs). My sight varies from day to day, and sometimes hour to hour, depending on tiredness, lighting, and stress levels, and whether I am in unfamiliar surroundings. So, what was easy yesterday, I may need help with today. I struggle to keep up with these changes myself, so there is no chance for other people, and most days I have to explain my needs to someone.

Purpose of this book

I am writing this book not to impress you, but in the hope it will create an impression. Perhaps it will give you a different view of life (pun intended!), perhaps it will help you better understand how to communicate and laugh with visually impaired friends or family members.

In the main chapters, I have added a Frequently Asked Question (FAQ) section as an easy way to give more information about my experience of living with a visually impairment and the natural questions many people ask.

At the end of the chapters, I have included ways I could help you to have more understanding and make a difference in your workplace, or change opinion on this kind of disability.

Every visually impaired person has a different experience, a unique story. This is my story and to some extent my husband, Martyn's, too. However, please do not assume everyone's journey is the same. I do not assert that I understand the experiences of other visually impaired people, but I do imagine there are some experiences which we all share - in particular, how other people relate to us.

I would like those with 'full sight' to understand how similar my life is to theirs. My passion is helping people, and if this book helps just one person, I will be happy.

I am no saint, and I don't want this book to be a sickly tale of triumph over adversity. I have not always been nice to be around, and at times I have made some poor choices about how to handle my disability.

Although I have been visually impaired for my whole life, my biggest challenges have come from my own attitude to my visual impairment. I hope, whatever challenges you face, you have the right attitude to come through them and live your best life.

This is my story for you to enjoy, regardless of the quality of your sight, to find it educational, inspiring, or challenging. Your experience may be the opposite of mine and you may disagree with my opinions. That is OK with me - if I have made an impression on you then my work here is done.

Amanda Harris (September 2022)

A Romantic Prologue

All I have to do is Dream.

The Everly Brothers

In the summer of 1957, 16 year old, Brenda Beeken was allowed to go on holiday with her best friend Gwen, aged 19. They spent the week in a caravan at North Landing in Flamborough, on the beautiful North Yorkshire coast.

In Brenda's words:

> "I was just 16 and about to enter the Lower 6th at Doncaster Girls' High School. I had met Gwen at a local church youth club and we became best friends. Gwen was pretty with jet black hair and a Snow White complexion. She was two years older than me and was a trainee nurse. At the end of August, our parents decided we were responsible enough to be driven to a caravan site at Thornwick Bay, near Bridlington and left there for a week's holiday together. We had a jolly time."

Staying on the same site were 17 year old David Bell and his two friends - both called Barry. Early in the week, the boys kicked their football across to the girls, who kicked it back, and a holiday friendship began. They were amazed to learn

Flamborough Friends

Back Row: David Bell and Gwen
Front Row: Barry Foster, Brenda Beeken and Michael Bell

that they all lived within a few miles of each other near Doncaster. The five young people spent the week together exploring the beaches and caves. When their week was over, they arranged to meet at a fair in Doncaster a few days later.

Brenda continues her story...

"The first week in September was always the Doncaster St Leger race week and we arranged to meet the two boys at the racecourse fairground. Gwen had also become smitten by a boy named Ian who lived in Flamborough. Both our fathers worked for the British Rail so we qualified for free rail travel. On the Sunday, after our holiday, we returned by train to Bridlington and met up for the day with Ian and his friend Graham who were both 18 and had motorbikes (ooh La La!). After returning Gwen picked up her bicycle from my house, said goodbye and cycled home. It was the last time I ever saw her.

I fell ill on the Tuesday and was in bed with the flu. On Wednesday, Gwen's brother cycled down to tell us the dreadful news, Gwen had died. She was the "first victim of the Asian flu in Doncaster". Later my mother would see this on the news placard in the town. I was convinced that I was going to die too and my parents were very concerned. My father was a kind and gentle Yorkshire man and I remember him telling me the day I recovered enough to go downstairs there would be our first television set waiting. I've been complaining for weeks that everybody had one except us! He kept his promise.

She Will Never...

Brenda and David's Wedding

The following Tuesday, my mother came upstairs to say she had just had three nice young men at the door inquiring about me. Of course, Gwen and I hadn't appeared for our fairground date so the boys remembering we'd mentioned our youth club, found the club, but were told the dreadful news and given my address.

My mother suggested they returned the following week when she was sure I would be well enough for visitors. I wasn't well enough to attend Gwen's funeral in September but was told later that two young men from Flamborough had ridden on their motorcycles to be there. I never found out how they knew about her death.

David's father ran a private hire car service and for several weeks after my recovery David, and his two chums, would drive up in a huge Austin 6 wedding car and the four of us would go to the cinema or a coffee house. Sometime in October, David arrived without the two Barrys and this was the beginning of our courtship."

Brenda and David were married in 1962.

In July 1969, they watched the first moon landing with great excitement... and nine months later I was born.

She Will Never...

Amanda's First Baby Photo

Chapter One
First Sight

*Aerodynamically the bumblebee shouldn't
be able to fly, but the bumblebee
doesn't know that, so it goes on flying anyway.*

Mary Kay Ash

The eye consultant wore an air of authority and a white coat when he said these words to my parents.

"She will never thread a needle."

"She will never drive a car."

"She will never fly an aeroplane."

I was only a few months old at the time but my parents remember it vividly and have often told me this story.

And so, it began - the emphasis on what I will never... or what I can't do. I have occasionally threaded a needle, with difficulty, to sew on a button and I once drove a car, but more of that in Chapter Six. I don't enjoy flying and I have no ambitions to be a pilot. As Meat Loaf sings, *"Two Out of Three Ain't Bad"*.

1

FAQ

Do your eyes look different to those of a *fully sighted* person?

If you look closely at my eyes, you may notice that they move constantly. I have no control over this, and I can't see it myself in the mirror. The only time I am aware of it is on video (or Zoom!). I sometimes have involuntary head movements to cope with my eye movement.

My eye movement is usually just a slight wobble, but when I am tired or stressed, they prefer a figure of eight. When I am speaking on stage, I imagine they are doing something akin to the Argentine Tango. I tell the audience not to worry, this is normal for me.

On an average day my disability is invisible. I have friends who are not aware of my poor vision until I tell them. I have friends who have known me for years who do not know about it. They get a shock when I ask them to help me to cross a road, or to read something for me.

So, if you want to see the world as I do, you will need to squint and move your head rapidly from side to side. Any volunteers?

I am sure the consultant's words were well meant. His intention was possibly to let my parents know that I would manage most daily tasks independently, there were only a few where I would need help.

He was probably unaware that my parents are classic car enthusiasts, and the idea that I would be unable to drive was devastating.

The consultant could have given this more positive message:

"She will be able to see your face."

"She will be able to read and write."

"She will be able to travel independently."

"She will be able to earn her living."

But... maybe he couldn't say those things for certain at that point. Diagnosis is necessarily based on the limitations of the tests available.

A dramatic birth

I was unaware of the drama of my birth. The clatter of the trolley and the echo of running feet down the hospital corridor to take mum for an emergency Caesarean Section, my dad's upset and fury at the delay which may have caused harm to both me and mum, or the joy of knowing I was alive and well.

I made my appearance in Doncaster on a Wednesday in April 1970, just in time for Coronation Street.

Thankfully, neither did I remember my first five days in an incubator in a room full of premature babies (also in incubators). At a healthy eight pounds I stood out from the rest even then. My mum was too ill to take care of me and

3

I didn't meet her until day six. My mum remembers the trauma of these first few days very clearly.

At first the doctors thought I may have some problems with mobility, as I seemed to be only moving one side of my body. This soon resolved itself and was possibly just laziness. But it was obvious from a few weeks old my eyes were not functioning as expected.

Nystagmus

The first thing the doctors noticed was my eye movement, called nystagmus, which is defined as constant movement or wobble of the eyes, which can be horizontal, vertical or circular. Consultants have observed on a bad day my eyes prefer a figure of eight movement - which is quite rare. I do like to be different.

People with nystagmus often have a *'null point'*. This is a direction in which the movement becomes slower or stops altogether. For me, this is downwards, and I read with the text tilted underneath my eyes - which makes reading an optician's eye chart quite difficult.

Nystagmus is a learned condition, but it cannot be unlearned. While there are some treatments which may slow the movement for some sufferers, there is no cure. It is often caused by the brain trying to cope with another eye condition. The primary cause of my poor vision is congenital optic nerve atrophy (now also known as optic neuropathy) which is defined as incomplete development of the optic nerves. Or to put it another way - there is nothing wrong with my eyes or brain, but I need a new USB cable to connect them. I have had a scan which showed clearly how thin and pale my optic nerves are.

At the time of writing, optic nerves have been grown in the lab, but it is not yet possible to make the somewhat complicated attachments to the eye and the brain. This may be possible during my lifetime, but I am likely to be too old to benefit, so there is very little chance of my sight ever improving.

Further complications

I also had a squint from birth - in my case this is my right eye turning inwards. A squint can often rectify itself as the child grows, but I still have mine. I will close my right eye when reading as this is when the squint is most pronounced.

There is no way of knowing what caused my visual impairment. It could have been a developmental issue during mum's pregnancy, or it could have been lack of oxygen due to my traumatic birth.

I have no other family members with a visual impairment and my condition was quite ironic, as my mum had taught in a school for the deaf before I was born. She was prepared to teach me British Sign Language, but this is not practical as I can't make out the intricate hand movements.

Baby with an *'off switch'*

At first my world was shapes and colours. This was the early seventies, so I remember a lot of yellows, oranges and browns. I would sit looking across the shiny yellow forbidden expanse of the kitchen floor to the blurry shapes beyond or would focus on the cream colour of my pram, rather than the fuzziness of the world passing me by.

At 18 months, I was given my first set of spectacles with a piece of elastic round the back of my head to hold them on. Until then I had not attempted to walk or even crawl.

Rescue on the Cliff Edge

In my blurred world I didn't feel safe to explore my surroundings, but now I started to move around the house.

My first crawl was (of course) at the top of the stairs. As the landing and stairs were carpeted in the same colour, I was unaware of the danger. Despite falling down the whole flight, I was too relaxed to suffer any harm. Maybe it is true what they say, *"What you can't see won't hurt you"*, but I am sure my mum's anxiety at seeing me roll down the stairs took a couple of years off her life.

My parents soon learned that removing my glasses would make me stay still. I had an *'off switch'*. Most parents would like one of those for their toddler!

I was in the waiting room at the eye clinic when I found my feet. This took my parents by surprise, and they thought it was another toddler in a similar furry teddy bear coat walking across the hard tiled floor.

There is nothing more unnerving for a parent than a toddler with poor vision. Once when we were out for the day with friends, I walked briskly towards the edge of a cliff and was only saved by the quick thinking of a family friend who caught me by the back of my coat.

Once I graduated from pram to pushchair, mum persevered until she found one where I would be facing backwards - towards her. Mum was close enough for me to see her, and this was preferable to the whirling blur of the world ahead of me.

I was registered as partially sighted as a young child. This simply means I was on a register held by the local authority. Registration is voluntary and confidential but allowed me to access support and benefits, where appropriate. There

She Will Never...

Amanda's First Birthday

Young Book Lover

was the option for me to be registered as blind but my consultant chose the softer option, as I have a lot of useful vision. (I always smile at the American term *'legally blind'* - are there US citizens who are illegally blind?).

Throughout my life, I have been careful to avoid injury and my only broken bone was a toe - more to do with alcohol than poor sight.

The joy of stories

Nursery school memories are of a blurry blue floor and nipping my finger in a toy mangle (outdated even in the 1970s), and the magic of story time. We tiny tots would sit on the carpet with our fingers on our lips and the teacher looking down on us from a chair. I couldn't see the books on her knee, so didn't know how many there were, hoping for two stories today. I can still conjure the click and creak of the hardback picture books. I assumed the other children could only see vague colours and shapes on the pages. I was happily unaware of my difference. My parents read with me at home, but at nursery there were so many books - here my lifelong passion for stories began.

While my glasses helped with distance vision, they restricted my close vision (this is still the case with my contact lenses today). But I discovered that without my glasses on I could read any size of print if I held it close enough. Soon I was reading everything I could get my hands on, from *A Bear Called Paddington* to *Wind in the Willows* and from *My Naughty Little Sister* to *The Borrowers*. By the age of twelve, my favourite book was *Pride and Prejudice* by Jane Austen. I would escape frequently into a fictional world.

Television allowed me to explore the planet. It was my only chance to see a bear, a whale, or a dragonfly, or even a sparrow, robin or blackbird for myself. But best of all was the thrill of tiptoeing into the exciting dark of a cinema, with everything on the screen being larger than life. The first film I saw at the cinema was *The Rescuers* at the age of seven, and I remember the plot and songs to this day. I still feel the guilty pleasure of sneaking into the cinema alone to immerse myself in a story.

The house of adventures

When I was four, my parents were house hunting in Campsall - a small village a few miles north of Doncaster. They drove up to a derelict house, with a gap in the exterior wall large enough to let daylight through. My mum was not impressed, but my dad had fallen in love with it. Before they could get a mortgage for the cost, they had to find a local builder who was prepared to make it habitable.

Some would say this was an inappropriate environment for a small child with a visual impairment. To me it was exciting. As well as the wind whistling through the walls, the only running water was a standing tap in the kitchen and in the middle of the sitting room floor was a complete car engine. The previous owners had been eccentric artists and had left spooky artwork painted directly onto the bare plaster walls - a white horse in the dining room, but creepiest of all, a blackened dead tree on my bedroom wall. We lived in a caravan in the large garden for six months.

At a tender age, I was picking my way around ever-moving piles of rubble, scaring myself on the dark landing - which curved round half-way to conceal any monsters lurking in the shadows, and getting lost in the *'lawn'* with each blade of grass taller than me. It was the kind of house where adventures happen - and it spurred my imagination.

First attitudes

When I was young, I was sometimes told what I see is *'wrong'*. But what my eyes and brain tell me is my truth. I have had to learn not to be embarrassed if caught talking to a bag on the floor convinced it is the cat or running with my hand out to stop the bus, only for the bin lorry to whoosh past instead!

As with all children, my first knowledge of myself was formed by the adults around me. I had no choice but to agree when they told me what I would never do. My first memory of being different was moving more slowly than other children. This was very frustrating, and I took my frustrations out on my friends. I once tried to strangle a boy who had pushed in front of me at the slide. Looking back, I understand my actions. I knew that there was something different about me, but I didn't understand. It wasn't fair.

However, my classmates at nursery did not make assumptions about me. As we played, they realised something was different about me, but as young children do, they accepted me as I was. As we played, I realised something was different about me, and I was confused, upset and finally angry.

How can I help YOU?

I am a member of the Nystagmus Network®. I am happy to speak with parents whose child has a diagnosis of nystagmus or optic neuritis, if you know someone, do link us up.

Playtime

Chapter Two
A Brave New World

Disability is not a brave struggle or
'courage in the face of adversity.'
Disability is an art. It's an ingenious way to live.

Neil Marcus

Do you remember your primary school playground? If you close your eyes and picture it, what feelings do you experience? Excitement? Noise? Fun? Or anxiety and fear?

The wilds of the playground

To me, used to the familiar surroundings of home, the playground was a vast expanse of grey tarmac. I couldn't see clearly even a fraction of the way across. My classmates were fast moving blurs of colour. The noise of laughing, shouting, singing and squealing children meant I couldn't use my hearing to orientate myself. I stood at the edge feeling lost and scared. I dare not run in case I tripped over an unseen obstacle, and I couldn't find my friends if they ran away from me.

This was only a small local primary school, but I had never experienced such a crowd. I was not aware of any other

13

FAQ
How far can you see?

You are probably only asked this question by opticians and driving instructors. Have you ever thought about it? Next time you are outdoors, take a moment to look around you and notice how far you can see. Is there a distance you can see clearly and are there some indistinct images further away? Now squint your eyes half-closed. This will impair your vision and blur the details in the distance. You may be coming close to seeing the world as I see it.

I don't mind being asked how far can I see but it is tricky to answer for several reasons:

> I don't know how far you can see. My vision has always been poor, so I can't compare my view to yours

> My level of vision changes from day to day, sometimes from hour to hour, depending on my level of tiredness, stress, the lighting conditions - or for no reason at all.

> As I look around me to form a response, my annoying nystagmus perceives this as a test, and my eye movement tends to increase.

My usual response is that on a good day, with my contact lenses in, I can read line three on the optician's eye chart. Does that help? How about, if asked by the driving examiner to read a number plate, I'd reply, *"Is that red blur a car?"*

14

Most of what I see are shapes and colours. There is nothing wrong with my brain, and to make up for my visual impairment, it tries to fill in the gaps for me - which is not always helpful. As I navigate a bustling pavement, surrounded by blurry people, my brain gives me the face of someone I know for every person I pass, based on the overall shape and the hair colour. Sometimes it gives me the face of a famous actor or TV presenter. In fact, when I have met famous people in the flesh they have never looked as much like themselves as the pictures from my helpful brain. I was once shouted at by *Kenneth Williams* on a train (true story) - I didn't recognise his face despite having seen him many times on television - but the voice was unmistakable! The poor man was faced with a long line of schoolgirls wanting autographs. He signed some photos but when it came to my turn he had had enough. He put his pen down and shouted, *"NO MORE!"*.

I have long since given up believing the evidence of my own eyes and will not usually approach a friend in the street in case my brain and eyes are playing tricks on me. I can never trust what I see.

If you know me and see me in the street - please come up and say hello. My brain should then recognise your voice and stop trying to be helpful. Better still, tell me your name (this is more because of my current menopause brain than my visual impairment).

The Wilds of the Playground

children with disabilities at the school, there were certainly no others with a visual impairment, and no wheelchair users, and as this was the 1970s there was no education about difference or varied ability. My mum worked at the school part time as a Special Needs Teacher, so there were clearly other pupils who needed some support - but to me, this just meant every time I fell over or misbehaved, my mum was suddenly there - which didn't help with my classmates' opinion of me.

My level of sight was my *'normal'* and although I had been told I was 'partially sighted' I could not imagine what others could see. I still struggle with this - over 50 years later.

So, I believed the running, jumping, and skipping shapes around me saw the world as I did, and I marvelled at their courage.

I have a vivid memory of standing in the middle of a ring of *'big boys'* (they must have been about seven years old, and I was five). They were all chanting *"Spaz"* (short for spastic - an offensive term for a disabled person). They were pulling faces and jerking their arms and legs to mimic what they thought a disabled person should look like. I was upset and terrified. I had no idea that I could just have pushed my way out of the circle and escaped, but I could not see what was beyond them and I was scared.

The chaos of the cloakroom was daunting, and I would rather carry my coat around all day than fight my way to my peg. Each peg had a different coloured picture above it, but this didn't help me. I would talk about this to anyone who would listen, and I soon had some friends who would hang up my coat for me. I learned an early *'life'* lesson:

17

I could get what I wanted by making people feel sorry for me. I didn't have the knowledge or the language to explain my difference to my classmates - and they were too young to understand or care - but they were soon fetching pencils and tidying my desk for me; I enjoyed the attention.

I made a few good friends (who I am still in touch with today); life became easier. Dawn and Julie were my bodyguards in the playground, so I started to enjoy playtime. I remember we always played *Charlie's Angels* although I had not seen a single episode of the programme! I discovered I liked to be the peacemaker of the group and help others when I could. Though I admit I wasn't always pleasant to be around.

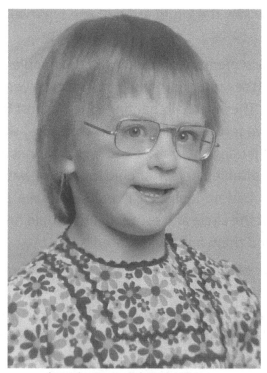

'Bottle-Bottom' NHS Glasses

Again, I showed frustration and violence at times. I once threw a clock at a classmate, and I hit a friend with a skipping rope handle. Those were the days I really regretted mum being on the scene so quickly.

Although mum drove to the school each day for work, as I grew older, I wanted to walk there with my friends (to stop off at the sweet shop!). I started to learn to cross roads using my hearing as well as my sight and enjoyed feeling I was one of the group.

From glasses to contact lenses

One of the reasons I was teased in these early school years was my *'bottle-bottom'* National Health Service (NHS) glasses. They were ugly and so thick I had a permanent nose-bruise. But they also caused me to have headaches, nausea and dizziness - which I now know to be eyestrain. Each lens of my glasses was concave, with the prescription in the middle, but my eye movement meant my perception was constantly flitting between the centre, the outside and the frame.

When I was five years old, my wonderful eye consultant, *Mr Palmer*, suggested to my parents that I try a brand-new technology called *'contact lenses'*. These would move with my eyes and allow me to stay focussed and have full peripheral vision. In 1975, fitting contact lenses to a young child was revolutionary, I was one of the first children in the world to try this - I was a trailblazer.

I did not appreciate this historical significance. I was terrified. I remember lying on a hospital couch in a blurry white room, with the smell of disinfectant and a scratchy white paper cover underneath me, with six people holding me down to try and insert a lens into my tightly closed eye. With my glasses off, I could see nothing except the large, rough male finger approaching my eye. I screwed my eyes tight shut and struggled and screamed. The lens never touched my eyeball and all I had to show for it was a sore eye and a headache. Maybe this paragraph has made you squirm - I am aware of many adults who are terrified of anything touching their eyes - well imagine it as a five year old.

Eventually, the decision was taken to insert my contact lenses under general anaesthetic. This seems a bit drastic when I look back on it now, but it shows the consultant believed the lenses would make a major difference to me. I only have a vague memory of waking up with the lenses in. Of course, nowadays, this would be a YouTube video called, *'Child sees mum for the first time!'* but for me there was no life-changing revelation. The anaesthetic made me sick and I dare not admit my sight was much clearer with the lenses, as I would then have to go through the awful process of insertion and extraction again. But I now had full peripheral vision and no bruise on my nose. I could no longer be called, *"Specky four eyes"* at school.

For reasons of practicality, my first contact lenses could be worn constantly for several weeks, but I dreaded the next visit to the hospital.

Down the drain

My first pair of contact lenses had been in for several weeks when my primary school teacher decided to get out the modelling clay. This was before the colourful stuff of today, instead it was grey, slimy and foul smelling - but being tactile, it was one area of art I could participate in fully. After an hour of messiness, I was at the sink washing my hands, when I rubbed my eyes, and both lenses came out and disappeared down the plughole.

I was determined not to admit the loss of my lenses to my parents. I hated having them put in. I remember riding my bike round the house after school and swearing blind (pun intended) the lenses were still in. But my parents knew better and that evening, the school caretaker unscrewed the U-bend from the sink. I don't know what he expected to find - certainly not a pair of wearable lenses!

Needless to say, I was soon back at the hospital having another pair of lenses put in under general anaesthetic.

As I got older, my fear of the anaesthetic became greater than the fear the approaching finger, and by the age of seven, my parents were putting in the lenses for me. My dad also encouraged me to put the lenses in his eyes. Now I am a parent, I realise how he could overcome any fears to do the best for his child. I don't ever remember him flinching.

I was soon wearing daily lenses and I learned to take them out myself. But at the age of eleven, with secondary school looming, I decided to learn to insert them myself. Without telling anyone my plan, I remember sitting in my bedroom with its flowery wallpaper and posters, and the view of the local colliery, in front of a magnifying mirror, bringing the lens close to my eye. After around an hour the lens was still on my finger and my eyes stung with tears of frustration.

Then inspiration hit me. My consultant had told me to use a mirror to put in my lenses, and I was trying to follow his instructions. All my efforts were focussed on using the mirror, but without my lenses, my reflection was just a blur.

So, I moved away from the mirror and used touch alone - and soon both lenses were comfortably in my eyes. I went down to tell my parents what I had done. Of course, they were very proud of me and relieved they wouldn't have to go through the trauma of inserting lenses every day. I have never looked back! (I really must stop with the puns.) Putting in my lenses is now so normal I am not aware of the process.

Although contact lenses improved my confidence considerably, I still had the same overall level of vision, and I still didn't understand how much I was missing out on compared to my fully sighted classmates.

I understand many people with nystagmus wear glasses all their lives, but for me, contact lenses were life changing. I only admitted this point many years later of course. This is why I have put a lot of emphasis on this historical story in this book. I am sure the process would be very different today for a child in the same situation.

Music

For my seventh birthday, I was given a bright red ITT Pony Radio (a colour I can see distinctly!) and pop music became my passion. Like many children my age, I lived for the *Top 40* on *Radio One* on a Sunday evening and made countless mix tapes on D90 cassettes using my Panasonic radio/cassette player.

I know what you are thinking - surely all visually impaired people will appreciate and enjoy music. With one sense impaired, your other senses will be heightened. This is not true for everyone. My husband has been visually impaired since birth; he has almost no appreciation of music. He can't pick out a beat and does not remember melody or lyrics like I do. There is no causal link between visual impairment and enjoyment of music.

Counting the leaves

By the age of ten, I was doing well academically at the small village school. My wonderful teacher, Miss Wadsley, expressed her concerns that I would not cope at the large local comprehensive school. On a visit there, my parents witnessed the head teacher being almost bowled over in the playground by the boisterous students when the bell rang - with no consequences. We all agreed I would not thrive in such a place.

My parents made the big decision to send me to private secondary school, for which I am eternally grateful.

In order to identify what support I would need at my new school, my parents applied for a Statement of Special Educational Needs to be issued by the Local Education Authority.

The application process included an assessment of my sight by Children's Services. In the 1980s a Statement of Special Educational Needs set out the needs of the child in education and the help that the school should provide. These needs were reviewed every year. The assessment was a gruelling process for the whole family, but my parents felt it was necessary to ensure I would get appropriate support. This process has now been replaced with the Education, Health and Care (EHC) Plan, which identifies all the needs of the child, not those purely relating to education.

I will never forget my meeting with the Social Worker. Using her many years of experience, she soon realised I was either in denial about my level of vision or didn't know the extent of it. I had been protected from the outside world. She decided to show me how poor my sight was compared to hers.

She asked my parents to leave the room and then the conversation went like this:

> Social Worker (looking out of our front window): Can you see the house across the road?
>
> Me: Of course, I can! (Well, I could see the shape and colour and knew it was a house.)
>
> Social Worker: Can you see the downstairs front window of the house?
>
> Me: Yes (by squinting, I could just make out the blurry shape of the white window frame against the red brick wall).
>
> Social Worker: Can you see the plant on the window sill.
>
> Me: Er... yes... (A downright lie.)
>
> Social Worker: I can count the leaves.

At this point I started to cry, and the social worker left the room. I thought at the time she had been very cruel, but I now appreciate what she did for me. Nobody had ever pointed out to me before the difference between *'fully sighted'* and *'my sight'*. I have forgiven her, but never forgotten her. This approach would probably be frowned on now, but it worked for me. She started me on my journey to acceptance.

A new perspective

My new-found knowledge made my young explorations harder. It was embarrassing to be with my friends, knowing just how different my level of sight was to theirs.

As a young child, I didn't respond well to this new information. I remember playing catch with the children who lived next door to me. I didn't catch the blue rubber ball for the whole afternoon - the colour blended in very well against the lawn. When my friends had gone into the house, I picked up the discarded ball, and threw it as hard as I could into the adjoining overgrown field. This was my way of getting rid of some of my frustration, and of having some control, but it might also have been spite - as I knew the ball would be hard to find in the long grass.

Unfortunately, I had forgotten my friend could see me through her kitchen window, and it was no use me denying what I had done. I was ashamed, upset and frustrated.

With my Statement of Special Educational Needs completed, it was time to move on to secondary school. The physical requirements were in place, but like many eleven year olds, I was still led by my extremes of emotion.

How can I help YOU?

I visit primary schools to give entertaining talks or workshops to children to motivate them to overcome their own challenges. This can be through a talk in assembly or some activities in class. Please feel free to contact me if you would like a visit to your school.

First Day at Wakefield Girls' High School

Chapter Three
Have You Got The Parcel?

One always overcompensates for disabilities.
I'm thinking of having my
entire body surgically removed.
Douglas Adams

In September 1981, I started at Wakefield Girls' High School. My journey from Doncaster to Wakefield each day involved thirty minutes on the train, and a walk through an unfamiliar city. Up to this point, my furthest journey had been to the local village shop. In the summer of 1981, I had my first experience of *'mobility training'*.

This consisted of practising the journey with a social worker and learning the best route to school, and how to cross each of the roads safely. I was also given a *'symbol cane'*. (This is a short white cane, which does not touch the floor, but alerts other people to my poor vision.)

Carrying this cane makes my invisible impairment more visible. I know for many visually impaired people the symbol cane makes them feel more confident and empowered to ask for help and they would not dream of going out without it. But at the age of eleven I enjoyed

27

FAQ
Can you drive?

No, I am not allowed to drive a vehicle on a public road. Are you offering me a lift? If so, the answer is, *"Yes please!"*.

I grew up around cars. My paternal grandfather ran a private hire car firm and my mum's father owned and repaired cars and motorbikes. My parents had taken part in 24-hour rallies before I was born, and our home garage had an inspection pit (with very clear markings so I didn't fall into it). My dad was often to be found under a car. I have very fond memories of his orange MGB in the 1970s.

I am not sure at what age I became aware I would never drive. I do know it has been one of my greatest disappointments and challenges. The modern world is designed for those who are lucky enough to own a car.

A few years ago, I got excited about the advent of driverless vehicles. But understandably, the law states that at least one occupant of the car must hold a full driving licence, so sadly this will not be the answer for me.

being different/contrary/stubborn/all of the above!

I hated my symbol cane from the start. As I have said, it does not touch the floor, so can't be used to locate obstacles and it leaves me with only one free hand. I felt as if I had a sign round my neck reading *'disabled and incapable'*. I used it for the training and then it stayed in the bottom of my school bag for several years.

I still have one today in a cupboard somewhere. I last used it around five years ago when I went to see the comedian *Adam Hills* at a gig and wanted to get to the front of the crowd to meet him afterwards - I find a sharp tap on the leg will move people out of the way!

Crossing roads - with or without help

I struggle to judge distance and speed of oncoming cars, so crossing roads was very challenging. Even now I will go a very long way to avoid crossing a busy road. I use my hearing when crossing a road and I worry the new electric vehicles will be silent and deadly.

The road outside Wakefield Station was a particular challenge for me and the social worker helped me to choose the best place to cross and how to use my hearing as well as my sight to cross safely. She then crossed the road herself and left me to do it on my own. As I stood there brandishing my symbol cane and waiting for a gap in the traffic, a helpful pedestrian came up to me and took my arm, helping me across the road. I couldn't bring myself to tell her I needed to cross on my own to complete my training. This happened twice before I crossed unaided. Here is a life lesson - always ask if someone needs help before offering it - even if it seems obvious.

By the way, I will always accept help to cross a road, now I am not being assessed and providing this is the road I want to cross!

Special Note to reader: If you are driving and see me waiting to cross the road, where there is no official crossing, then please do not stop for me. I cannot see you waving or flashing your lights, so I don't know whether you have stopped for me. This can be dangerous if you have stopped for some other reason and then move off again without noticing me. It may feel like the right thing to do as a driver, but I do not appreciate it.

Have you got the parcel?

There were approximately thirty girls who made the train journey with me to the High School each day (and about the same number of boys travelling to the nearby boys' school - but we didn't talk to them!). I always had someone to walk with and I soon got to know those in my year. I was still not confident crossing the roads and I asked the other girls to help me. Children can be cruel, I remember them walking in a group ahead of me, only noticing my presence when they approached a road. Then one of them would say, *"Have you got the parcel?"*, meaning me, and someone would grab my arm to cross the road. I felt at times as if they didn't see me as a friend, more as an inconvenience.

Dealing with my impairment .... Not

As I have previously mentioned, as a youngster I often did not deal with my impairment well. On my first day of catching the train home, I had been introduced to a girl in the sixth form, called Sarah, who had offered to walk with me to the station after school. She said she would meet me in the library. I knew there was a school library, but I wasn't sure where it was, I was scared of walking in there and not being able to find Sarah. I had visions of crowds of tall sixth formers all looking identical in their school uniform - all laughing at me.

My last lesson of the day was Music, I told my teacher of my problem. She gave me directions to the school library, but I couldn't bring myself to say I would be embarrassed looking for Sarah there. So, I took the easiest (and most foolish) option. I told her they were to meet me in the city library, which was next to the station! I don't know why she believed me, but she walked me there anyway. Of course, I could then get to the station on my own. Having avoided one potential embarrassment, I then had to explain what I had done to Sarah on the train, to my parents when I got home, and to the other teachers who had been looking for me! It was not a good start.

Teenage growing pains

As this was my first taste of independence, I learned very quickly how embarrassing visual impairment is as a teenage girl. I don't see facial features well - there is not much contrast in the human face, regardless of skin tone, so I would often rely on hair colour and shape to recognise the other girls. I was astonished at how often my friends would experiment with new hair styles and colours. They soon learned to re-introduce themselves to me after a visit to the hairdressers.

Most people develop their own personal style during their teen years, but here was another area where I lacked confidence. I knew from an early age I don't see colours in the same way as others. Pastel shades look grey to me, and so I prefer bright colours - whether they suit me or not. I am oblivious to what other people are wearing, so I don't get a sense of fashion.

Clothes shopping is challenging for me. I can't pick out items from across the room and need to get close to everything to see it. Looking around is difficult while I am concentrating on where I am going, so I am very slow and soon get frustrated. I like to choose clothes by the feel of the fabric. I was certain I looked different from my peers, but this was the eighties, so I have some wonderful photographs of me with huge, permed hair and very large shoulder pads (no doubt looking just like every other teenage girl of the time).

Makeup was even more of a challenge. By its very nature it is supposed to subtly enhance facial features. To me, my friends looked no different whether wearing makeup or not. I was sometimes shocked when a girl was punished for wearing makeup at school - I couldn't see it. I tried to experiment with makeup, but I was always conscious, if I could see it, I was probably wearing too much - was I more clown or lady of the night? Badly applied eye makeup would stick to my contact lenses and cloud my vision, or worse could irritate my eyes.

Embarrassment is a severe teen affliction (my son tells me he could die of it!). As I used my eyes more, I started to make involuntary head movements - I assume to mitigate the eye movement. This is apparently common with nystagmus, but it added to my fear of seeming strange.

Left back in the changing room

I made a few friends at Wakefield. We mainly bonded over books of course. They introduced me to fantasy novels. Our favourite was *The Belgariad* by *David Eddings*, and we formed a *'secret society'* where we each took a role from the book. I avoided the sporty girls and those who were interested in boys.

There were some advantages to being my friend (other than my sparkling personality of course!). I was allowed to eat with the older girls at lunchtime, to avoid the rush to my dinner sitting - and I was allowed a friend to go with me (my friends had a rota for this!). I was never punished for being slightly late for lessons, and neither was my companion.

The best perk for my bookish and non-sporty friends was during hockey. Triple games on a Wednesday afternoon was the bane of my life, and I was obviously a danger to have around on the hockey field. But the teachers didn't want to treat me any differently so they would ask me to play the *'left back'* position on the better team, so I would never see any action during the game. This was boring and very cold - hockey was often played in the snow, wearing only our Aertex shirts, short gym skirts and the obligatory grey gym knickers. One of my friends would usually be at *'right back'* and invariably at some point during the match one of my contact lenses would mysteriously *'fall out'* and my friend would have to go back to the changing room to *'help me put it back in'*. This could often take around an hour in the warm pavilion with a drink. As contact lenses were so rare in the early 1980s, the teachers didn't challenge this - at first.

But after a while the teachers worked out this ruse, and from then on, I wasn't allowed to play hockey. Instead, I had to run round the pitch for the whole of the three hours. I probably deserved that!

Strangely, I enjoyed playing tennis. With both myself and my opponent standing within touching distance of the net, I was sometimes able to return the ball and I had a powerful serve.

Another visual aid

Alongside the symbol cane, I was given a monocular to help me read the blackboard. As the name suggests, this is one eye of a pair of binoculars. While this was very useful, it only enabled me to read one word at a time. I soon developed good friends who would share their notes with me!

I thrived on the discipline of the school routines. There were archaic routines like *'Wednesday bells on a Friday'*. (Assembly was usually longer on a Wednesday, which changed the times of all the other lessons hence *'Wednesday Bells'*. We didn't change the name when this happened on a Friday!) Once a week lunch was cheese slop and beetroot! Cheese slop was a cross between a quiche filling and an omelette - it looked disgusting with the purple beetroot on top, but it tasted delicious.

I loved the school building. As usual my most vivid memories are not visual ones. I remember the smoothness of the curved wooden bannisters and the smell of wood polish, the echo of the gym and the sound of girls' feet on the floor of Jubilee Hall where we went for assembly each day.

Boys are only after 'One thing'

The headmistress, Miss Hand, was from another age. She called us, *"Gels"* (pronounced with a hard 'g' and to rhyme with bells) and warned us of the boys who lurked outside the school perimeter waiting to pounce on any girl who strayed too near.

"Gels", she would announce, *"Do not sit on the wall next to the road. There may be boys walking along the pavement, and boys are only after one thing."* She never explained what the one thing was, but she gave me a fear of the opposite sex that stayed with me throughout my time at the school.

One morning, in my first year I was sitting on the raised balcony at the back of the hall for assembly. I couldn't see Miss Hand on the stage at the other end of the room, but the girls around me started sniggering when she walked onto the stage. She took a deep breath and enunciated, *"Gels, this thing has been found on the school field. I hope none of my Gels know anything about it!"*

I nudged my friend, *"What is it?"* I hissed.

"A used condom," she giggled.

I didn't know what a condom was, but I joined in with the laughter anyway.

A summons from the Headmistress

Shortly after this, I had a message from my teacher that Miss Hand wanted to see me. I had never been inside her office before but had heard the myths of punishments doled out there. I was terrified and couldn't think what I had done. In the corridor outside Miss Hand's office, were three hard back chairs where girls would wait to be summoned. But

The Headmistress' Office

the most frightening aspect for me was the *'traffic light'* system on the jamb of the door. I had been warned by the other girls that entering while the light was red would incur a punishment. I had to put my face very close to the faint set of lights before I could see that the red light was on. I crouched there without blinking until the light turned to green. I knocked and heard a strident, *"Come!"*.

When I opened the door, all I was aware of was the intricately designed tapestry rug stretching out before me and wood panelling on the door and walls. The room smelt of wood polish and flowery perfume and was so large I could hardly see the desk at the other end. I walked slowly forwards across the rug, worrying I was adding to my misdemeanours by treading mud into the impressive carpet. When I finally reached the desk, I stood patiently. When Miss Hand looked up, I could see she was smiling. She had called me there to give me a *Commendation,* a certificate from one of the teachers for good work. I can't remember the details of the award, but I was determined never to do anything to deserve a punishment in the awful and awe-filled room.

Drama queen

By the age of eleven, I had decided I wanted to be an actress. I had started taking the Speech and Drama exams set by the Royal College of Music at age six - by which age I found I could memorise poetry easily - my first learned poem being *Cats* by *Eleanor Farjeon*. (I can still remember the words to this day) I progressed through all the grades. Each exam consisted of a learned poem, or later a Shakespearean monologue, and some improvisation.

Learning the lines was easy, but props could be trickier. While practising *Viola's* monologue from *Twelfth Night*, I had placed a ring on a piece of white paper on the floor so I could easily pick it up. But I had no way of knowing what the floor covering would be in the actual exam. Luckily it was a wooden floor, and I didn't have a problem.

My preferred style of learning has always been auditory and if I listen to something enough times, it will stay in my brain forever. I can remember song lyrics from the 1980s better than I remember what I had for dinner yesterday!

In 1982, I entered the *Barnsley Music Festival* with a mime. I wouldn't enjoy *Marcel Marceaux* as his act is completely visual, but I didn't need to see to do mime myself. I could choose from several titles and picked *'The Cupboard'*. My mime was of walking into a dusty closet and finding mum's clothes - including a ring that was too large for my finger, and a pair of high heels in which I pretended to totter around. I won my class! I was asked to perform in front of an audience at Barnsley Town Hall that evening. I loved it! I couldn't see the audience, even the faces on the front row were blurred, and I made my parents sit at the back, where I definitely couldn't see them. This was the first time I experienced the sheer adrenaline high of being on stage. It is still my drug of choice.

Looking through my drama certificates, there is one where the examiner had marked me down for my eye movement. Another examiner told me, *"You will never look good in a screen test unless you can keep your eyes still"*. I took this to heart, my dream faded, and I decided to concentrate on my studies. I was not picked for school plays - my only acting credit at school was *'Woman 3'* in a play whose title

I can't remember, and it was years before I would tread the boards again.

Creating the drama

I have always enjoyed being the centre of attention. At primary school my mum was there, and I was praised by the teachers for my work. Whereas, at Wakefield, all the girls had passed the entrance exam, and they were all finding their way in the world, with me just being a minor curiosity. I couldn't keep up with their stories of life outside school and so I invented one of my own.

What I am about to write I am not proud of, and I deliberated long and hard over whether to include it in the book - but I want to make it clear just how far I have come in confidence and social skills since that dark time.

At the end of my first year at Wakefield, we had a photograph taken of the whole school. As one of the youngest girls, I sat on the floor at the front. The oldest girls had to stand on benches at the back. It was a blazing hot day and one of the sixth formers fainted in the heat. Friends and teachers rushed to help her. I wanted to be that girl.

On the way back to the classroom, I pretended to faint. The first time, people believed me, and I got the attention I wanted. It became a habit to lie to my friends about illness but the more I did it, the more *'addicted'* I became. As I got older, my friends were gaining more independence, they were telling stories about discos and boys, so the amount and seriousness of my lies escalated. I felt I had to have something to contribute to the conversation. By this point I was enjoying more fantasy novels, so as well as the lies about illness, I decided to tell my friends I was telepathic and could communicate with people in America! They didn't believe me, but they sometimes humoured me.

I firmly believe this behaviour was my way of coping with my visual impairment. I felt my life was boring in contrast to my friends, I could not start a conversation about the world around me, as I could not trust what my eyes were telling me.

I remember one day after faking illness at school, one friend told me I deserved an Oscar! I felt hot with shame but couldn't stop the lies - my truth felt too boring to be part of any group in the school. What I didn't realise at the time was I was driving my friends away. Some of my friends still tease me about it to this day.

Teenage Years (Fourteen)

When I was fourteen, the awful but expected day came. I was in my bedroom doing my English homework, an essay about a picnic, (strange what the brain retains). I heard the phone ring downstairs, and a few minutes later my mum was shouting me to come down. One of the girls who travelled on the train with me was so worried about my *'illness'* she had told her mum, who had rung my mum.

My parents were confused, hurt and angry. They asked me *"why"* but I couldn't tell them. By this point, I couldn't explain it to myself! But it was all over. As a punishment my parents removed all my beloved posters from my room. I was mortified at school and at home. It was one of the darkest times in my life - deservedly so. I am sorry to all of those who had to put up with me as a young teenager.

Work experience

I must have been around fourteen when we were all encouraged to approach employers to gain a week's work experience. I had no idea what type of work experience would prepare me for being a star of stage and screen. I somehow ended up at a care home for older people.

I can't remember how this happened. A couple of other girls were also working there for the week, I remember the walk to the large red brick building. I was very nervous - I worried about the lighting and recognising the people. What if I couldn't do anything to help?

But what happened was worse than anything I had pictured. We were all shown into a large, dark room with a high ceiling to wait for the *'matron'*. The room reminded me of Miss Hand's office, with its ornate dark wood furniture and an oriental rug. I was very nervous.

After a few minutes a middle-aged woman entered and asked haughtily, *"Which one of you is Amanda Bell"*. I identified myself. *"I am sorry dear, but we have just found out you are partially sighted. I can't allow you to work here. I have rung your parents and they are on their way to pick you up."*

The matron swept out of the room, followed by the other girls. I convinced myself that this would be the pattern of the rest of my life. I remember crying on the journey home and seriously believing I would never have a job.

No job for me

I struggle to differentiate coins, so never had the confidence to get a Saturday job in a shop, as many of my friends did. I didn't earn money for myself until I was much older. I remember a week's work experience in a large, well known retail store, where I stacked shelves for a week, as I was not trusted on the till. I soon knew what I didn't want to do for a living.

I hope that attitudes to young people with a disability have changed since the 1980s. At that time, I was never asked what I could or couldn't do - decisions were always made based on the assumptions of strangers. I didn't have the confidence to argue at that age.

My inner negative voice

In my teens, my inner voice changed from, *"She will never..."* to *"Everyone else can ..."*.

At first it was, *"Everyone else can see properly"*. This was probably true of the girls at my school, but it meant I didn't consider the issues and challenges faced by other people. I spend a lot of time in taxis and like to talk to the driver. A Pakistani taxi driver once told me there is a saying in his home country, *"If you stand on your roof, you will see all your neighbours' houses burning".* In other words, everyone faces challenges in their lives, even if these are not visible.

I soon progressed to, *"Everyone else looks better than me."* I can only see the basic outlines and colours of what everyone else is wearing, but my lack of confidence in choosing clothes became more frustrating as I got older.

The worst one was, *"Everyone else is having more fun than me".* The chatter in the school corridors as we got older was about discos and boys, pranks, and weekend sleepovers. I lived eighteen miles away from most of my school friends and was not invited to the sleepovers or shopping expeditions. However, I now realise this was a Catch-22 situation. It was obvious to those around me I was feeling sorry for myself, and this did not encourage the girls to become my friends.

Going out in the evening has always been challenging. I am almost completely *'night blind'* which means I see almost nothing after dark. Also, my eyes take much longer than those of a *'fully sighted'* person to adjust to a change in lighting. Coming out of a brightly lit building into the dark means I have no sight for a few minutes.

In my first term in the sixth form, a large *'L-Plate'* appeared on the common room wall at school, and each girl who passed her driving test would write her name on it. This felt like a personal insult. Of course, *'Everyone else'* was learning to drive and I would never do this. However, I was prepared to take advantage of one of my friends who learned to drive early and had a car!

Heartbreak at the disco

When I was fifteen, I went to a school disco with a trusted family friend. The dance was at her school, and I would know nobody except her, but we giggled as we got ready. For once I was prepared to enjoy myself. There would be boys. I wore a white top and silky slinky trousers which appeared to change colour from green to purple as I moved. I was very slim and had the latest hairstyle - I felt good.

My friend's parents dropped us off and I was so excited. I knew all the music of course. I was soon dancing and singing with a crowd of strangers. I discovered that I love loud music and dancing, but only when I have someone, I trust to help me when needed.

After a few minutes I met Simon, who asked me to dance with him. He was blonde with blue eyes and slightly taller than me. I had never danced with a boy before. We danced together all evening. We jumped up and down together to *Last Christmas* by *Wham!* We invented some crazy moves. The slow song at the end of the evening was *Saving All my Love for You* by *Whitney Houston*. We put our arms around each other swayed and kissed. I felt as if I was floating above the floor and the lights were magical. We had a final kiss and then it was time to leave. I arranged with my friend to go back the following week.

I daydreamed my way through the next few days and was so excited to see Simon again. For some reason we were late to the disco, and when we arrived, the music was pumping, and the lights were flashing. I had expected Simon to wait outside for me, but he wasn't there, and I sent my friend in to find him. She came back very quickly without him and said the words I have never forgotten.

"He has found out you are disabled, and he doesn't want to see you".

The rest of the evening is a blur. I sat by myself in the blare of music and flash of lights, not even being able to watch what was going on around me. I couldn't see across the room, and I was worried about bumping into Simon and his mates. I was sure they were all laughing at me. I stayed at my friend's house that night and cried myself to sleep. I knew I would be alone for the rest of my life - I was unlovable. I can't hear any of the music from those two discos without being transported back to this incident. Isn't it strange how music can do this?

Microscopic issues

I did well in my O Levels and decided I wanted to study Biology, Chemistry and Maths for A-Level. My teachers were not so sure. Once again, I was called to Miss Hand's office - this time with my parents. The conversation was a familiar one.

Miss Hand: I understand you want to take sciences at A Level. However, your teachers tell me you can't see down a microscope.

Me: Yes, I can - I did well at Biology O Level.

Miss Hand (with a gentle smile): Your Biology teacher is aware that your friends have been covering for you for years and telling you what they see. This won't work at a higher level.

So, at the age of seventeen, after two terms in the sixth form at Wakefield, my parents took me to visit Worcester College for the Blind. The question was, would I need to move away from home to achieve my potential?

How can I Help YOU?

I provide talks, Q&A sessions and workshops for secondary school students who are facing challenges. I understand how hard it can be to feel different at that age and how this can lead to behaviour which is unhelpful.

Do you know of a secondary school who would appreciate this kind of talk?

New College Worcester, ©NCW
(Formerly known as Worcester College for the Blind)

Chapter Four
Small Blind Boys Can Be Tactile

In the country of the blind,
the one-eyed man is king.

Proverb

By the end of my initial visit to Worcester College for the Blind, I had fallen in love with everything about it. I remember sitting at a motorway service station with my parents on the way home where they asked me very gently for my thoughts. I didn't need to think twice. I wanted to be there.

No limits

Two weeks after my seventeenth birthday I left home and moved across the country, from a girls' school to a boys' school! The college was in the process of merging with the National College for Blind Girls at Chorley Wood, but when I arrived, there were around one hundred boys, but only eight other girls there - all in the sixth form.

The headmaster was a wonderful man called Bob Manthorp. On my initial visit, he had welcomed us with schooners of sherry for my parents (in the middle of the day with no thought for the drive home!), and chocolate biscuits for

FAQ
Can you read Braille?

No, I have never tried to learn Braille. Reading Braille is as challenging as learning another language. Each character represents a letter, or a word, and the reader must have enough sensitivity in their finger ends to feel each tiny dot. Writing Braille involves a very large and noisy machine which punches the holes into the thick Braille paper. The Braille machine looks like a typewriter with nine keys. Therefore, reading and writing Braille are two distinct skills.

The reason I have not learnt Braille is not through laziness. I have enough useful vision to read large print. As you are asking, my favourite font is Arial Bold 22.

Which looks like this.

Most documents are not in this font, so I carry a powerful magnifying glass with me at all times. I have reading glasses to wear over my contact lenses, but my eyes move outside the frames a lot. The strength of the magnification can give me a headache.

I used to love reading for pleasure, but I now find audio books easier. When my son Matthew was at primary school, his teacher told us he was very good at reading out loud with varied intonation. This was because he was used to having his bedtime story read by Stephen Fry or Miranda Richardson!

With the advent of talking devices and smartphones, Braille may be a dying art.

me. When I arrived there to stay, he called me into his office and warned me to be careful as, *"Small blind boys can be very tactile."*

He was right. The young boys would run along the corridors of the building, usually singing or making aeroplane noises to let others know they were coming, and if they bumped into one of the girls *'accidentally'* then their hands would explore our contours with no embarrassment - it was their way of *'seeing'* us.

All the students were boarders and ranged in age from 8 to 19. There were very few who had any useful sight, and suddenly I was the sighted one.

I first lived in a room on the girls' corridor which I shared with Jane, who was petite and blonde. Her boyfriend Gary (who lived on the boys' corridor on the same floor) was over six feet tall and dark skinned. They were both totally blind. Their first question for me was, *"Can you read the instructions on this packet of Angel Delight?"*

When I said that I could, with magnification, they decided that I could stay! I was *'delighted'* to be asked to help. They were so different in appearance, but they could not see each other. Gary obviously sensed me noticing this and he said casually, *"Yes, I know I am a big, black, blind, bugger!"*

No joke about sight was too irreverent.

At Worcester, I lived in an inclusive community and became aware of the social model of disability in everyday life.

The 'Social Model of Disability'

I love this explanation of the social model of disability by *Fleur Perry* in her excellent article *Social Model of Disability; Who, What and Why?*

> 'The social model of disability is the concept that disability results from the interaction between a person's characteristics and their unsuitable environment - not their medical condition. An environment filled with barriers will create a significant difference in experience for a large number of disabled people. Conversely, an inclusive environment will offer the minimum level of intrusion for the experiences of all but enable disabled people to live their lives equally.
>
> To improve the experiences of disabled people, you don't need to medically *'fix'* everyone, but to think practically about what the goals are and removing environmental barriers.
>
> Put simply, disability is the experience of being a square peg in a round-hole world. And the world is changeable.'

I am very lucky to have experienced living in an inclusive society for two years, where not only were the barriers removed, but I had more useful sight than other students.

The magical world of Worcester College for the Blind

My two years at Worcester were magical. In my first weekend there, I played pool, pedalled a tandem with a young blind boy on the back, and had a trip to the West End to watch *The Phantom of the Opera*.

No sport or activity was out of bounds. There was blind football, played with a bell in the ball, on a concrete pitch with netting at the sides to keep the ball in play. Some of my fellow students went on to be part of Team GB on the blind football team at the Paralympics.

I have never been a football fan, my favourite activity was archery, which took place in the garden at the college. Even with no useful sight, it is possible to be a competent archer - all you need to know is the exact position of the target. My job was to evict the headmaster's dog from the garden before we started, and to help find the wayward arrows in the long grass, usually using my feet.

On my first night at the college, I played pool in the common room before someone suggested going up to their room for *'Sticky Fingers'*. This turned out to be the local pizza delivery service - to my relief. I had never heard of having pizza delivered, soon I was sitting on someone's bed in a room with ten others, talking and laughing together. There was one boy sitting in the corner by the door who seemed to have as much sight as me. He kept nipping out of the door and back again - I later learned he was keeping track of the Snooker World Championships. His name was Martyn, I thought he was rather cute.

As I arrived in April, I had a term before starting my A-Level course. I used this time to learn to touch-type (even the eight year old boys could type faster than me), additionally I had Biology and Maths lessons. Most of all, I joined in with as many new activities as possible!

Haylee and Perkins Brailler - Paths to Literacy.com

On Friday nights, a group of us were taken to Birmingham to learn to canoe in a swimming pool followed by *McDonalds* on the way home. I enjoyed this experience, I soon graduated to a canoe on the River Severn - very cold and wet and never to be repeated! I swam in the school pool at any opportunity. I could take out my lenses to swim as collisions with other swimmers was acceptable. There were trips to the cinema, theatre, bowling and so much more. Anything was possible, and I took advantage of everything on offer.

Useful sight

The culture at the College was to teach us to make full use of what *'useful sight'* we had. So those of us who could read print - of any size - were not taught Braille.

It goes without saying I could no longer use my disability as an excuse or to make myself stand out from the crowd. We were taught that we could do anything we wanted to. I was told that one student had become the world's first blind astronomer (with Braille star charts)! A blind boy who was two years older than me at college is now an International Political Correspondent for the BBC.

Classes were in very small groups - there were four of us in my Biology A-Level group and eight of us in Maths and English. Handwriting was discouraged (as it was often illegible) so depending on our level of sight, we either used an electronic typewriter, or a Perkins Brailler.

Braille was not used for exams - with blind students either typing, with someone to read back for them, or using a *'scribe'* to handwrite for them. In the 1980s, the technology was not yet developed for computers to *'speak'*.

Meeting in the Rain

Biology and ... Chemistry

The College didn't offer an A-Level course in Chemistry, so I was preparing to study Biology, English Literature and Maths.

Initially, I had lessons on my own with the Biology teacher Mr Brown. I enjoyed these lessons, the science equipment was all accessible to me, and Mr Brown made me laugh.

After a few weeks, Mr Brown told me that another student would be joining me for the lessons - his name was Martyn! Of course, Mr Brown knew I liked him, and I am sure he decided to have some fun with us. For the lesson where Martyn was due to join us, I dressed carefully in very 1980's fashion - a white blouse and a long lemon skirt, with my long hair down my back.

I arrived early for the lesson and was horrified when Mr Brown gave me a trowel and some plastic bags telling me to go out into the school grounds to collect soil samples which we could test for acidity. It was raining. Martyn found me crouched by a flowerbed, covered in mud with water dripping from my nose and my hair. He laughed at me, we carried the samples back to the lab, where we flicked water at each other from the water bath. I can't remember analysing the soil samples. I am sure Mr Brown was more interested in matchmaking than Biology practical - I soon forgave him.

Mobility again and McDonalds

When I arrived at Worcester, I had to go through mobility training again (with the hated symbol cane). I resented this. I had been travelling to Doncaster on the bus on my own for years, now I had to prove I was safe to walk into

Worcester from the college. One of my tests was to catch a train to the next stop on the line and come back again. It was not overly testing after my seven years of train travel from Doncaster to Wakefield! I 'aced' it!

Early in the Autumn Term, I was finally given my 'green card' to say I was allowed to go into town by myself. I was so excited. I had a Biology lesson in the morning, but the rest of the day free to finally explore on my own.

There were four of us in the Biology lessons now - Martyn and I had been joined by two girls who were both totally blind (so no curb on our messing around). I was eager to leave the classroom at the end of the lesson, but Martyn stopped me before I could get out of the door.

Martyn: Where are you going?

Me: Into town.

Martyn: Can I come with you?

Me: No! I have just got my green card. I am going on my own.

Martyn: I'll treat you to a McDonalds...

Me: Oh, alright then.

Clearly, I could be easily bribed! This was our first date, which was followed by our first kiss. We have never looked back! We have now been together for over 30 years.

Martyn was honest with me from the moment we met that he could lose his sight - but we were teenagers, we were untouchable, immortal and in love - nothing else mattered.

Martyn had been at the college since the age of fourteen and knew how to make the most of our time there. It was he who took me out canoeing on the cold river and taught me archery.

It was during this time I first realised how much I enjoy helping others. As we had a lot of useful sight, Martyn and I were often asked by the other students to take them shopping. I remember guiding three blind girls at once through a crowded shopping centre on a Saturday in search of the latest fashions. On the annual trip to *Alton Towers*, we were trusted to go off on our own. As students from *'The Blind College'* we had been given passes to jump the queues, we spent a whole hour going round and round on the log flume until we were soaking wet and dizzy.

As sixth formers, we were encouraged to cook for ourselves. Martyn did all the cooking for both of us on a tiny *Baby Belling* in our sixth form kitchen. We were given a food allowance each week. Martyn and I pooled our resources, which meant we could shop in the food hall at *Marks and Spencer* and afford a taxi journey once a month to the local Italian restaurant (we had moved on from the *Big Mac*). The restaurant was called *Heroes,* it was small and friendly and didn't take bookings. One memorable Friday evening we turned up to find it had closed down. The taxi had left, we had no mobile phones in those days, so we had a long walk back to school for *Sticky Fingers*.

All the sixth form students also received benefits payments, as we were classed as *'unemployable'* until we had mastered the necessary life skills taught at the College.

She Will Never...

Prank - Table on the Roof

Prank - View of the Table

Fun and pranks

The blind boys enjoyed playing pranks on each other and the staff. The term before I arrived at the college, a table disappeared from the dining room, and was found on the flat roof of the boys' bedroom corridor. It was still set for breakfast. The only way it could have got there was through a small window. Even now, Martyn claims he had nothing to do with this adventure - but he would have been a very useful lookout, and he took the incriminating photographs.

Water fights were common in the girls' and boys' corridors, often with us all blindfolded to make it a level playing field. These were banned once we moved to the newly built sixth form block with its plain blue carpets.

Visual impairment and relationships with others

In the sighted world, my visual impairment has a major impact on my relationships with others. Fully sighted children and adults can learn to do a task by watching others, whereas I often have to be taught to do the simplest of things. Fully sighted people will start a conversation based on what they can see. I will never start a conversation with *"Look at that...."* As a young person I was very conscious my conversation was limited to past events, rather than what was around me at the moment.

All of this changed at Worcester, so I could form deeper relationships with those around me. I learned that my abilities are far greater than my disabilities. This was much more important to me than my A-Level success.

In Love

The first proposal

When I was eighteen, I flew with Martyn to his home in the Isle of Man. This was the first time I met his parents. Martyn had done this journey many times, but it was very daunting for me. The flight from Liverpool to Douglas only takes 25 minutes but I felt ill on the flight and then arrived among strangers. Martyn's parents drove us to their home in Peel, where I was greeted by their dog, a large German Shepherd named Elsa, who ran at me and pinned me to the wall with one huge paw at each side of my head. In ten seconds, my slight fear of dogs disappeared. She only wanted to play, and she was the best dog I have ever met. Martyn and I took Elsa for long walks in the beautiful countryside - we had time on our own at last.

However, after a couple of days, there was a telephone call from Stoke, where Martyn's paternal grandma lived. She was very ill in hospital. I accompanied the whole family back to the mainland (this time the four-hour journey via boat, my first experience of seasickness). We stayed in Martyn's grandma's bungalow, I shared the one bedroom with Martyn's mum, while Martyn and his dad slept in the sitting room. The bungalow was freezing, and I remember sleeping in my clothes and gloves, with an itchy tartan blanket for extra warmth.

One night, while on our own in the bungalow, as we were cuddled up on the sofa for warmth, with no preparation, Martyn simply asked, *"Will you marry me?"*.

I had no hesitation, but my answer was, *"Not yet"*. We had been together for just over a year, but from this point on we saw ourselves as an engaged couple.

Sharing my experience

During our time at the College, Martyn and I visited the local secondary school where we spoke at the assembly about visual impairment. Everyone in Worcester was used to seeing *'the kids from the blind school'* around town, and it was important we were somehow integrated into the community. This was my first experience of talking to an audience about my disability and I loved it. The students were amazed our disabilities were not obvious - neither of us carried a cane and there was particular disappointment that we did not bring a guide dog (under 18's are not usually allowed to have a guide dog).

We did take a football with a bell in it, I remember rolling it down the aisle between the students and some of them trying to kick it with their eyes closed. I am sure the teachers didn't appreciate an impromptu football match breaking out in the school hall.

Two years later - moving on

The two years at Worcester changed me, and my perception of the world around me. I realised it was OK to ask for help, and I am not the only person facing challenges. It made me more adventurous. Also, I had fallen in love, which changes everyone.

I had not taken the time to plan my future. My only ambition was to pass my A-Levels and go to University. I needed a degree to prove the doubters wrong.

At the age of nineteen, I had an understanding that the world is set up for those with full sight, if I was to compete in a fully sighted world, I would need to find my own solutions.

I wasn't aware at the time but this would fit into the definition of *'The Social Model of Disability'*.

I had no idea what I wanted to do. There was still an outdated belief at Worcester that the best professions for the blind are piano tuner and physiotherapist. As I am tone deaf, and don't relish the idea of touching people's bodies for a living, neither of these were options for me.

I left Worcester College for the Blind in 1989 with three A Levels at Grade A and a fiancé. Martyn had been accepted at Nottingham Trent University to study Accountancy and I was heading for University of Leicester to study English Literature.

How can I help YOU?

My experience in the inclusive environment of Worcester College for the Blind gave me a real insight into *The Social Model of Disability* and that small changes to environment and attitude can make a huge difference to someone with a disability. I give talks and workshops to businesspeople and organisations who want to embrace the social model to ensure diversity in their workforce.

Island Boy

Chapter Five
Island Boy

I have never played for a draw.
Sir Alex Ferguson
(Former manager of Martyn's
beloved Manchester United)

Martyn has been my best friend, my most fervent supporter, my chef, my husband and my rock for over thirty years, so this book would not be complete without including his story.

He was born in Holywell, a small town in North Wales where everyone knows everyone's business. It was a home birth and apparently, at a few minutes old, he was held up naked at the bedroom window for the onlookers to see. He has never enjoyed being the centre of attention!

At one year old, he moved with his parents and older brother to the Isle of Man, where his parents ran a guest house and smallholding. While I was staying out of the kitchen at home, his parents needed both boys to help in the family business. So by the age of seven, Martyn was cooking bacon and eggs for the guests' breakfast, or hanging from the external metal fire escapes to paint

Martyn's FAQs
What is it like to have sight in only one eye?

What is it like to have sight in both eyes? I don't really remember.

Humans are predators and we have our eyes at the front but having two eyes means we can triangulate to judge the distance and speed of objects around us. So only having one useful eye makes crossing roads more difficult.

I have no peripheral vision to my right, so if I am walking with someone, I prefer them to be on my blind side for protection.

If I had full sight in my good eye, I would be able to drive - but this is not the case.

Why do your eyes look so different from each other?

My right optic nerve has been damaged beyond repair by the pressure at the back of my eye. The eye has effectively died. I am gradually losing my iris and pupil, my eye is fading to a pale blue. The white of my eye is often bloodshot as it becomes dry and irritated very easily. Also the pressure in this eye is very low, so it is *'squashy'* to the touch and looks as if it is sunken into my head. These differences don't worry me, but I realise that others can judge me on appearance alone.

Mine is a visible disability.

them. He had learned many life skills from a young age.

At the age of five, Martyn was suffering with terrible headaches, and was struggling to see the blackboard at school. He was diagnosed with glaucoma and despite his first eye operation, he had lost the sight in his right eye by the age of seven.

Glaucoma is a condition in which the fluid builds up in the eye which can damage the optic nerve, causing sight loss. It increases the pressure in the eye. The common test is the *'puff of air'* test you may have had at the opticians. Glaucoma is common in older people, but very rare in children. Due to this rarity, we had to fight to have our son Matthew tested for it when he was a baby, as most eye consultants have not experienced it in one so young.

Martyn's mother was diagnosed with glaucoma at the age of eighteen and was told there was a fifty percent chance of her passing it on to her children. Martyn's older brother, Andrew, is fully sighted. Famous people who had childhood glaucoma include the singers *Ray Charles* and *Andrea Bocelli*.

Martyn had been tested for glaucoma as a baby, but this test was erroneously done under general anaesthetic, which is known to lower the eye pressure, so the symptoms were missed.

His primary school experience was similar to mine, although he still wore his thick NHS glasses when we met at the age of seventeen. Martyn was subjected to physical bullying. On one occasion, a group of boys waited for him on the way home from school and beat him up badly. He managed to stagger home and told his mum who the ringleader was. His dad was working at the local quarry and apparently left work early to visit the boy's parents. He was angry and covered in the dirt and dust from his job, I imagine his threats were not idle ones. This did not stop the emotional bullying, but there were no more physical attacks.

At the age of eight, Martyn was hospitalised with acute Immune Thrombocytopenic Purpura - which caused internal bleeding and intense pain. He remembers having blood taken every two hours day and night while he was in hospital. The condition was life threatening at the time, he was prescribed corticosteroids for some time afterwards, which caused him to gain in weight in those sensitive teenage years.

Also, around the age of eight Martyn had his first Trabeculectomy operation to reduce the pressure in his left eye. (Please see the link in References: Glaucoma UK, Trabeculectomy Surgery for an explanation of this procedure, but be warned, this is not for the squeamish!) This is not a permanent solution, its effects usually lasting fifteen to twenty years. Most cases of glaucoma are in people over sixty, one such procedure can keep the glaucoma at bay for the rest of their life. Martyn has had two of these procedures at the age of fifteen and again in his thirties. His prognosis for keeping the remaining sight in his left eye was not good.

He went on to secondary school on the island, but at the age of fourteen he visited Worcester College for the Blind, and, as I did three years later, he decided it was where he wanted to be.

His first half- term holiday at the College, he chose to spend on an outdoor adventure course with other students, rather than going home. He had been a Sea Scout on the Isle of Man, and at Worcester he took up rowing on the River Severn as well as archery, snooker and pool.

Martyn first saw me across the crowded dining room at the college, on my initial visit. I must have stood out as a stranger in the room of familiar faces. He liked my long hair and can remember my striped jumper. I was unaware of him of course, in the noisy room full of children, we did not speak until my first night at the college three months later.

Love at First Sight

At the time I met him, Martyn only had sight in his left eye, but his sight complemented mine very well. My reading vision was better than his, whereas his distance vision was better than mine - we worked as a team. He also knew he would never be allowed to drive.

The younger boys at the College lived in dormitories, think *Hogwarts* without the four poster beds and the owls. The sixth form boys had either single or double rooms. While the few newly arrived sixth form girls had relatively spacious rooms, the boys lived in *'cells'* barely large enough for a single bed, a wardrobe and a built-in desk. Yet for some reason we always chose to spend time in Martyn's room - it could have been the lure of the *ZX Spectrum*. In our final year, we moved to the large Sixth Form Block with single rooms and a communal television room.

Due to his upbringing, Martyn's attitude to his sight was, and still is, very different to mine. He was blind in one eye and knew he was likely to lose the sight in his other eye eventually, but he has always been an optimist and threw himself into every possible activity.

We revised for our A-Levels together. Martyn would regularly leave the room to *'check on the cricket score'*. The first time this happened, I went to find him after an hour or so, happily watching the game. His unbelievable excuse was, *"They haven't mentioned the score yet"*. We were soon watching together, and I learned about the *googly* and *silly-mid-off* when I was supposed to be revising *Macbeth*.

After our A-Levels, he returned to his parents' new home in North Wales, I went back to Doncaster. I still have the typed letters he sent to me every day during this summer - I am not sure I was such a good correspondent.

One Thursday in August, we had to ring the College for our A-Level results after 09:00. I was sitting by the phone at 08:30, nervously looking at my watch, and had to dial several times before I got through. I then rang Martyn in great excitement. His mum told me he was still in bed and hadn't made the phone call yet. This sums up his attitude to life. The results would be the same whatever time he rang for them, there was no use worrying about them.

His attitude to life has never changed despite all that life has thrown at him. His motto is, *'If you can't change it, why worry about it'.*

To be continued...

Amanda in Paris

Chapter Six
Three A-Levels and a Fiancé

Disability is a matter of perception.
If you can do just one thing well,
you're needed by someone.
Martina Navratilova

During my time at Worcester, many of the *'old boys'* returned regularly for long visits. When I left, I began to understand why. Re-entering the sighted world was not easy. For the past two years there had been no need for me to explain my sight or to ask for help. I felt that my life would never be this way again and my confidence dropped for a while. It took me several years to find my feet and my passion.

In the summer following my A-Levels, I visited Paris with my mum. I fell in love with the city - the large monuments, tall apartment buildings, boulevards and, of course, the food. Notre Dame in the evening was beautiful even though I couldn't see the whole building. I started to believe that I can enjoy something visual in my own way. However, I would never be a true art lover. I used my symbol cane to get through the crowd to view the *Mona Lisa* (tiny!) but

FAQ
How do you cope?

I cope in the same way everyone else does.

I muddle along from hour to hour and day to day. I can accomplish most things in my own way - which often takes more time. It is tricky to give examples, as *'my way'* is so familiar to me. Here are just a few:

> I always close my right eye to read, as it moves to the centre when I concentrate.

> When crossing a road, I use my hearing more than my sight, so I often wait for all traffic noise to stop before I cross. Bicycles and electric cars can be dangerous.

> I have learnt the location of my favourite shops and it takes time for me to find them if they move. I tend to shop for clothes at the same places where I know the layout. I avoid some shops due to poor lighting or loud music. It is only recently I have taken to online shopping for clothes. I am lucky to be able to afford regular grocery deliveries.

> I often use my feet to feel my way, particularly if I am worried there may be a flight of descending steps ahead with no markings.

> When I enter a someone's house for the first time, I carefully count the steps up to the door, so (hopefully) I will not fall on the way out.

I avoid being out on my own after dark, as I will struggle even in a familiar place. Friends will often guide me by their elbow in the dark.

In a crowded room, I will stay by the wall, and I prefer others to come to me. I get easily disorientated in the middle of a crowd. If you see me, come and say hello.

I realise I am lucky enough to be able to pay professionals to do my gardening, cleaning and decorating. Not everyone has this luxury.

Of course, there are days when I get upset about my disability, but these are fewer as I get older. I am happy to laugh at the silliness of it all, I hope you can do the same with any challenges you face.

when it comes to impressionism, by the time I get close enough to see anything, it is just coloured dots! As with everything in life, I like it big and bold, I know a Van Gogh when I see it. I also love the feel of a cold marble sculpture.

I had no plan for a career, but I knew I wanted to study for a degree. After all, I had grown up with, *"She will never..."* I had been accepted by University of Leicester to read English Literature. This choice was based on my love of reading, and the fact Martyn was going to study Accountancy just down the road in Nottingham.

University of Leicester Pateroster

University Challenges

My first term at Leicester was one of my lowest points. There were other students from Worcester College in my year, but not on my course. Although they had less useful sight than me, they appeared to me to settle in easily. I did well academically but I found it difficult to enjoy the social activities of a traditional student life. I lived in halls with five other students. Although they were friendly, I didn't have the confidence to join in their fun. I felt alone and scared.

The university campus seemed very large to me. Even the building where I had my lectures was a challenge, as instead of a lift, it had a *'paternoster'* - a chain of open compartments moving slowly in a loop so passengers can step on and off at any floor. This was always busy - other students appeared to fling themselves on and off with gay abandon and climb up or jump down onto floors. My impression was the hated thing was always crawling with students, but I was scared of missing my footing. There were stairs too but some of my tutorials were on a very high floor and I was lugging heavy books. I did brave the paternoster a few times, but I often missed my floor. I couldn't judge when the compartment was level with the floor and often left it too late and had to use a couple of flights of stairs. Interestingly, this paternoster was one of the last of its kind in use in the UK. It was closed not long after I left, although it has been preserved for posterity.

To make matters worse some tutorials were held at the houses of lecturers. As well as studying I had to try to use a map to navigate the strange city. By December, I was not coping at all, this was when I suffered my first and only panic attack. I remember lying on the floor of my room thinking I was having a heart attack. Nobody was around in my hall, and I managed to make my way to the Dean's office. I tearfully asked him to ring my parents - I wanted to go home. Looking back, maybe I should have asked for more help from the tutors or the other students. It would have been useful to have someone to mentor students with a disability - I am aware that this happens more nowadays.

I felt that I had to try to be like everyone else and not be a nuisance, as most of the other students were away from home for the first time. It was not the right place for me at the time.

I know my parents were disappointed. I was diagnosed with nervous exhaustion and stayed in bed for a few days. I found the courage to make the difficult decision to leave the University.

My parents were concerned I might stay at home and do nothing, so my dad gave me a job in the print room at his company. I hated it - but I think this was his intention.

Print room work

The office was all male and they had been instructed to turn their girlie calendars to face the wall before I arrived. They told me this and I assured them I wouldn't be offended by the scantily clad models as I couldn't see them anyway. But I couldn't change the fact I was the daughter of the Managing Director - a spy in the camp. My job was to use the noisy and smelly print machine to copy drawings. But most of the day I sat in the corner with a book. It gave me time to think about my future.

As was to be the case so many times in my life, at the

lowest point I found the courage to make a big decision. While I was at Leicester, some of the other girls in my hall were studying Law and I had enjoyed listening to their conversations about legislation and cases. One evening, a job jumped out at me from the local paper - receptionist at Grainger, Appleyard and Fleming Solicitors in nearby Doncaster. Mum drove me there for the interview. She tells me I strode confidently up the stairs to the office in my new suit from Dorothy Perkins. I was offered the job.

First office role

I had never worked in an office before, but this small company was the ideal place for me to find my way round the challenges. First was the telephone system with its flashing lights for each line, and the small print list of extension numbers. Then there was the electronic typewriter (this was the 1990s!) with its small screen for error messages. My obsession with magnifying glasses started here. I typed up invoices, greeted clients and used the fax machine - even though I usually couldn't read the faint faxed documents. I learned very little about the law, but I did learn I could be accepted as a member of a team and earn money in my own right.

While nobody in the office (including me) was fully aware of *The Social Model of Disability,* I soon learned everyone in the small team was willing to help me. I was in control of the reception area, and I could produce documents in large print - there were no complaints.

At University I had felt worthless at times, and genuinely believed I may never be employed. My time at Grainger, Appleyard and Fleming Solicitors helped me to find a purpose.

The Proposal

A second proposal

Martyn and I were together most weekends - travelling between Doncaster and Nottingham by train. He had settled into student life really well and we spent our weekends at the cinema or playing pool at his local pub, *The Raven*, where we were forty years younger than most of the domino-playing regulars.

We were in Doncaster one Saturday when I spotted an engagement ring in a jeweller's window. We were not particularly looking for one, and jewellery displays are usually too small for me to see but maybe fate took a hand. The ring had (and still has) a beautiful pale sapphire which caught my eye. Martyn said something like, *"Shall we buy it then?"* - very romantic!

We were very giggly when we got home but told my mum all we had bought was the *Bran Flakes* she had requested. We were both a little nervous at telling my parents our news.

Later that evening, Martyn got down on one knee in our favourite Italian restaurant, this time I said, *"Yes"*.

We drank enough wine to have the courage to break the news to mum and dad. Of course, they were happy for us, and we celebrated properly with Champagne. We knew it would be a long engagement.

Martyn was honest with me from the beginning about the prognosis for his sight. He knew he could become totally blind one day. I know my parents had some concerns about how the two of us would manage on a daily basis, but they liked Martyn so much they couldn't really disapprove. As for me, I was young, in love and nothing mattered. When you are 20 the *'one day'* will never come. I was right not to

Behind the Wheel

Fast Driver

be concerned. I knew we were meant to be together. We are still both very romantic.

Martyn charmed my parents with his sense of humour. On his first visit to my house, mum had just bought a new washing machine. He read the manual and told her she would need to wait 25 minutes before opening the door after a cycle finished. Mum was furious and was about to complain to the store, when Martyn let her know, it was actually just 2 minutes. He still has a very dry sense of humour (I am certain he was involved in the dining table incident at college).

Coming of age

For my 21st birthday, I had a big party at the village hall across the road from our house. Family and school friends came and we had a great night. It turns out I enjoy the flashing lights and the dancing when I know everyone in the room, and I am the centre of attention - who would have guessed?

The highlight of my birthday celebrations was the present from family and friends who had arranged for me to have a driving lesson! They had found an instructor who was prepared to take me out on a local airfield in his dual control car.

From the moment I sat behind the wheel, I was grinning from ear to ear. The instructor started by asking me what I could see ahead of us and was very relieved when I could see the tractor parked just to the side. He explained the pedals and I was off - soon driving at over 70 miles per hour. I turned the car round by myself and then he again asked me what I could see. There was something blurry

Driving Experience

ahead of me, but I couldn't quite make it out. He grinned and told me the blur was my dad's car. He suggested I did not drive quite so fast on the way back!

I have a lot of photos of this day. I look so excited and happy. My life would be so different if I could drive, I am sure I would be an excellent, albeit fast, driver! I vowed I would do this again one day. It should have been for my 50th birthday, but COVID intervened. I plan to arrange this very soon.

Decision to leave University of Leicester

Looking back, my decision to leave University of Leicester was right for me at the time. In many ways it was the opposite of the safe environment of Worcester College - which is ironic really, as most of the students at Leicester were living away from home for the first time. I needed to find my own path, which took me a further two years, during this time I gained some valuable work experience.

In 1991, I followed Martyn to Nottingham Trent University to study Law.

How can I help YOU?

There is far more support for disabled students at UK universities now, but I can provide training and workshops for staff, students and student unions on adjustments to help disabled students to settle in to their new environment.

Happiest Day

Chapter Seven
Coursework and Confetti

No pessimist ever discovered the
secret of the stars, or sailed to an uncharted land,
or opened a new doorway for the human spirit.
Helen Keller

Martyn and I moved into a large but mould-ridden flat in Nottingham in September 1991, and I started my degree course. Our flat was a four-minute run from the Law building, so I often rolled out of bed very late.

I found I had a passion for Law. It is logical and has a link to past traditions. There were no blurry blackboards, and instead I would sit in a light and airy lecture theatre. We studied several subjects each term, the work was challenging, and I was ready for it.

My favourite topic was Criminal Law (Donoghue v Stevenson - the snail in a bottle of ginger beer, I will never forget). Tutorials were in the same building as the lectures and I revelled in the cosy atmosphere of the tutorial rooms, where ten or so students would have an informal chat with the lecturer.

FAQ
Do you listen to the television?

Please do not watch your language around me (see what I did there?). I watch television. I can see things from your point of view, and I do have a vision for my business.

I don't want you to feel awkward or embarrassed around me - my language is the same as yours.

As mentioned in the introduction my sight has never changed but the politically correct terms have evolved throughout my life. I will never be offended by the language you use. However, this is only my opinion - others with a disability may have a different viewpoint. I am definitely not alone in my view, just look at the popularity of the Channel Four programme, *The Last Leg*.

I find it embarrassing when others are socially awkward around me but try to put them at ease.

One of my worst experiences of social awkwardness happened many years ago at the makeup counter of a well-known store in Nottingham. I was looking for my usual colour of foundation but was struggling to read the labels. Often, I don't ask for help as I find it hard to identify a member of staff. I was interrupted by the sales assistant asking if she could help. Her tone was bright - she was about to make a sale. I explained I am partially sighted and asked if she could find the bottle for me. Her attitude completely changed. She came round the counter to me and touched me on the elbow. She spoke to me as if I was a five year old, as she gently manhandled me away so she could search the counter.

"Don't worry." She cooed, *"I will do this for you."* Then I heard her tone of panic.

"Can you use cash or a card machine? Do you need some help with that?" Between gritted teeth, I explained I would pay by card and, rather than appear rude, I allowed her to move me over to the card machine and explain how it worked as if I had never used one before.

I would hope customer service training in that particular store has improved, but I now buy my cosmetics online (it is much easier for me to find what I want there anyway).

There was no frightening paternoster, but no lifts either. The building was only two stories high, and the stairs kept me fit.

In the early 90s, most students would handwrite assignments, but because I had my Statement of Special Educational Needs, Doncaster Local Education Authority provided me with a PC - first a BBC B and later the 286, 386 and 486 - which are now listed on a website called *'Ancient Computers!'* I had a printer with an endless supply of paper (in a concertina fold with holes down the edges) and toner. I have a good typing speed and could produce work very quickly. Martyn had the same, and we would sit side by side working. It seemed to me Martyn had far fewer lectures than me - a Law Degree leaves very little time for socialising which suited me.

I was allowed to record lectures on a Dictaphone and friends soon learned if they had missed a lecture, they could borrow my recording! I don't believe I ever missed a lecture, I won the Sweet and Maxwell Prize for most promising student at the end of my first year.

Nottingham - my home
I enjoyed living in Nottingham, where I soon found my way around, discovering the best places to eat, and becoming a regular at the local cinema. We went to the theatre when we could afford it.

I have now lived in Nottingham for over 30 years and know my way round very well. You would be surprised at how quickly I walk down the street. However, I am very slow in unfamiliar areas or where I think I can see an obstacle. Often, the obstacle is just a shadow on the pavement, but

I will slow down just in case - sometimes to the annoyance of those around me.

I grew up in a small village with two buses a day (one to Doncaster and one home). Even I can't fail to see a double decker bus approaching, so catching it was easy. Nottingham is a large city with many buses, I learned the difficulty of reading bus numbers. At even a short distance 8 and 9 look the same to me. I learned the places each bus visited and could see the outline of the destination on the front of the bus or count the letters. Later, Nottingham City Transport changed to different colour buses for different routes, which was amazing. I learned all of the colours and no longer had to squint at every bus as it went by. At university, and later at work, I was the go-to person for which bus to catch. Perhaps my colleagues saw me as a bit of an *'bus route anorak'* but knowing routes was very important to me. It was a way I could be independent and helpful to those around me, two things which always make me happy.

University social life

The social side of university life was still a challenge, and I didn't have the emotional skills to adapt to it. I hadn't yet learned it is OK to be different. It seemed to me everyone else was out clubbing or drinking every night, and I struggled to find like-minded friends. I realise now that living with Martyn may not have helped with this. The other students may have seen us as a couple and assumed I didn't want to be involved with other activities. Martyn had the friends he had made before I arrived.

Even when I was invited to the pub, I was nervous. Spotting my friends in a dark smoky room was difficult, and I felt awkward asking them to meet me outside. I still lacked the confidence to ask for the help I needed.

As I have said before, I don't see facial expressions and therefore often miss out on nuances in conversations. I felt awkward and embarrassed around my peers.

If I know you really well, I might recognise you from a distance by your gait, or the colour of your hair. I remember being able to spot Martyn at the other side of the Market Square in Nottingham just by his walk and his jacket.

I believed there was something wrong with me because I didn't enjoy nightclubs or smoky pubs. Cigarette smoke has always irritated my eyes and in those days, there was plenty of it. A lot of my course mates smoked, but I wouldn't even take a drag of a cigarette.

I struggled with when and how to tell people about my challenges. Most of the first-year students were away from home for the first time, I was anxious not to appear *'needy'*. I tried to fit in. I dabbled a bit with the drama society but to be honest I didn't have the time to fit this in around my studies.

I became painfully aware of how my lack of vision affected my conversations with new people. While travelling in a car, I don't receive the visual stimuli of the scenes passing by. As mentioned before, my conversations never start with, *"Look at that..."*. So, when finding things to say, I will often go back into my past, or the weather or television.

Work and university

Throughout my first two years at university, I worked casual hours in the filing room at Berryman and Co Solicitors in Nottingham. My job was to go through the thousands of archived files and either destroy them or mark a date for their disposal. It was not the easiest job for me, with the faded papers and the dust, I often had eye strain by the end of the day, but I enjoyed having access to all of the historical documents. I would sometimes be there on my own for a day, then it would be my job to find any archived files needed and take them down to the relevant department. I got to know everyone, I even occasionally had an outing to court - which I loved.

My course included a *'sandwich year'* where students worked for a Law firm, and as I was part of the furniture almost, I was offered a sandwich placement by the partners of the firm. They treated me as if I was fully sighted but would give me any help I asked for - exactly what I needed.

I spent most of the year in the Criminal Department, including supporting a barrister at a murder trial. I will never forget the crime scene photographs - some things cannot be unseen. I accompanied the solicitors to police cells and on prison visits. I soon found my way around the Magistrates' court and other solicitors would ask me to run errands for them. As usual, I wanted to be independent and didn't tell my colleagues about my visual impairment.

At the time, the Magistrates' Courts in Nottingham were in a Grade 2 listed Victorian Building and the court rooms themselves were wood panelled and dark. Many a time I walked into the wood benches which blended in so well with the walls and floor, but I didn't make a fuss about it, and neither did anyone else. I was accepted as I was.

She Will Never...

Graduation

First Home

Martyn had graduated before my sandwich year and started work for the Legal Aid Board. We had moved out of the damp flat and were renting a small house on a main road with the bus stop right outside the front door. It was a lovely little house, but the people on the top deck of the bus could look into our bedroom window and the buses ran late into the night. We wanted to get on the property ladder.

We travelled by bus to view houses - we would need to live on a good bus route anyway. There was one house I fell in love with. It was a former council house with large rooms, in a good area of Nottingham and we had been offered a mortgage. We had arrived there by bus, but when it was time to leave, we realised to catch the bus back, we would need to cross a major road - which was a challenge to both of us. I remember my tears of frustration when we got home - imagine not being able to buy your dream home, for want of a pelican crossing!

In the end, we bought the house next door to where we were renting. It was a compromise, but it was ours.

Wedding day

Later that year was our wedding day. I may have mentioned I like being the centre of attention, and I had looked forward so much to standing in the church doorway with everyone turning round to look at me. However, as dad and I walked down the aisle, I realised Martyn was still facing forwards - he was not looking! Was he not interested in seeing me in my dress? I know I am coming across as shallow here, but I had been looking forward to this my whole life. When I reached his side, he asked me to hold his hymn book while he put his contact lens back in. It had fallen out just as I

Hold My Hymn Book

reached the church, so he would not have been able to see me if he had turned round. I did toy with the idea of going out and coming in again. But of course, I gave him plenty of opportunities to say how lovely I looked as the day went on.

My parents were so happy and proud of us. They had now known Martyn for seven years and realised we made a good team. My mum enjoyed the organisation. My dad had undergone heart surgery six weeks before the wedding, and was too emotional to complete his speech - so of course I stepped in. It was unusual in 1994 for a bride to make a speech, but I wanted our wedding to be different. Martyn's *'best man'* was female (so we had already started to buck the trends).

Our wedding day was truly one of the best days of my life. Back then it was not common to have a wedding video, so I had decided just to have a photographer. A family friend offered to video the day for us as a surprise. No doubt he thought we would notice him lurking around with his (enormous) video camera - but of course we didn't. It was a lovely surprise when he gave us the video a few days later. We still have it - now transferred to DVD. I know I shouldn't be surprised at how close the camera was to us, without either of us noticing. All of the shots are of the side of my head - but it makes it more natural somehow.

Finding a job

I wanted to specialise in Employment Law, so during the last year of my degree, my course mates and I applied for training contracts with solicitors, who would sponsor us to undertake the Legal Practice Course needed to become qualified as a solicitor. Out of over sixty applications I sent out, I had two interviews. The first turned me down because I would not be able to drive. The other stated they thought I would not get a good enough grade. I could have made a complaint to either of these firms, but I didn't have the confidence, and I also didn't want to start my legal career on a negative note. Besides, many of my classmates were also struggling to get a job.

In 1995, I passed my Law Degree with a 2:1. I became Amanda Harris LLB (Hons). I had no idea what to do next.

Future employment

I signed on with a temping agency, but I struggled with being in a different office each week. The worst day was spent inputting data at a desk in the middle of a large warehouse. There were noisy machines moving at speed around me, I remember being scared to leave my desk, even to go to the toilet.

However, I got good feedback everywhere I worked, and I finally landed a six-week placement in HR Admin for a local college. The office was small, and I got on well with my five colleagues. They took my disability in their stride. After about three weeks, my manager called me in and told me how impressed she was with my work. She handed me an advert for a permanent full-time job in HR for Nottinghamshire County Council, and suggested I apply for it.

The Disability Employment Act 1944 was in force at this time. This Act set up a quota system requiring employers with 20 or more employees to ensure that at least 3% of their workforce were disabled people. The job I had applied for was ring-fenced for disabled applicants. It may even have used the old-fashioned word *'handicapped'* in the job description. When I turned up for the interview, I met with the mother of a friend of mine, her daughter had much less useful vision than myself. She was clearly waiting for her daughter to come out of the interview and had her daughter's guide dog at her feet. To my astonishment, she glared at me, and in a loud whisper urged me to not go for the job as she felt I had a much better chance of getting it than her daughter.

Thank goodness times have changed. This was the first time I realised fully how difficult it was in 1996 to get a job as a disabled applicant. The council quota scheme guaranteed every disabled applicant an interview, but it was often the *'least disabled'* applicant who was successful. Thankfully the law has now changed. I was offered the job.

How can I help YOU?

This is a shout-out to all HR departments and employers, contact me for presentations about DDA or how your organisation can work with diversity to ensure disabled people are welcomed into your workplace. Or indeed how you can add training for staff dealing with customer service to meet the needs of visually impaired or blind people.

Be careful what you wish for,
lest it come true.

The Old Man and Death - Fables of Aesop

Chapter Eight
Climb To The Summit

I have a disability, yes that's true,
but all that really means is I may have to
take a slightly different path than you.

Robert M Hensel

For the next fifteen years I worked in large HR teams for the two local councils. I soon learned that I had no choice but to make all of my colleagues aware of my challenges from day one. This was not easy as in my first few weeks at each new office, I faced new challenges each day.

On my first day in that first job, my new manager met me at reception and took me into an office. She asked me what adjustments I would need to do the job. While I appreciated her intention, I found this difficult to answer. I had not seen the office I would be working in, and did not have a clear idea of what my duties would be. I remember mumbling something about needing good lighting and maybe a larger screen, but I had no idea really.

My first role was in an old building with long dark corridors. There were frosted glass windows to the offices on either side, but these were mostly blocked by files, so there was

FAQ

What is the worst thing about your disability?

Most of the time I don't think about my disability, I just deal with each challenge as it arises. But here is a list of the main issues which can upset me and give me a *'bad'* day:

> Not being able to drive. Our society is constructed for those who can travel quickly and easily and when meeting new people there is an assumption I can drive. I don't always find it easy to ask for lifts but will always accept them if offered. My worst experience was picking up my son Matthew from primary school one day. It was raining heavily, and the teacher knew we would be walking home. She asked the other parents whether anyone could give us a lift (it was less than five minutes' drive). One parent offered us a lift, and I thanked her. She responded by saying, *"I am only doing this because of the weather, don't expect it every day!"*

> I have found some people make assumptions about those who use public transport - either it is due to poverty, or they are making a sacrifice to save the planet. I could afford to run a car, and while I believe in conservation, I would own a vehicle if I could drive. I deserve neither the censure nor the

praise implied in these assumptions. I would love a large car, with some power under the bonnet. After all, I am the daughter of two car enthusiasts!

My disability is embarrassing. I can come across as awkward or standoffish at social events, as I find it hard to work out what is happening, and I am sometimes anxious about what others think about me. But I can usually look back on embarrassing moments and see the funny side.

My disability is invisible - people sometimes assume I have a learning disability, or I am drunk.

I don't know what I don't see. My visual memory is really poor, and I don't remember routes and places. But also, I could not accurately tell you what the outside of my house looks like or describe the faces of my parents and closest friends. I don't feel people's faces.

no natural light. The walls of the corridors were green with wood panelling around the doors. The names on the doors were on gold plaques - very difficult for me to read as there is no contrast. The overhead lighting was yellow and dim. I soon learned the way to my office, to the ladies and to the communal kitchen, but apart from that it was a case of leaning down and peering at the names on the doors.

Merely walking down the corridors was embarrassing. They were long and straight so I would be aware if someone was walking towards me, but could not identify them until they were almost passing me. I didn't know whether to smile or greet them, and I would keep my head down. Once the person approaching me was my manager, who ducked into her office before I could speak to her about the urgent papers in my hand. When I reached her door, I realised she was in a meeting.

I had to explain that it would not be a good idea for me to carry a tray of drinks down these corridors and there were managers who did not take well to me refusing to provide refreshments for their meetings.

Three years into my role, my manager put in a request to change the lighting in the corridors to help me (and everyone else). However, when I left this role two years later the project was still wrapped up in red tape and never happened.

Photocopiers in the 1990s were better than they are today. They had large buttons to press - often brightly coloured. These days I struggle with their small screens and codes.

My first role in HR involved arranging meetings, writing letters, and a lot of filing. The filing shelves were my nemesis. Moving shelves stacked floor to ceiling with thousands of paper files each with a tiny tab stating the employee name. I could read the ones at eye level, but above and below me I had to pull out files and hold them close to identify them. There were a couple of memorable occasions where I worked as a team with a colleague who used a wheelchair. He would spot files for me, and I would reach files down from the top shelf for him.

I learned to find my own way of working. Learning the layout of the small-print forms that needed to be completed by hand, so I did not have to read them. Similarly with the computer screens which were of course green on black. This was my first experience of emails - which I much prefer in black on white.

Old challenges return

As soon as I began to work full time, I started with eye strain again. Eye strain affects different people in different ways, but for me, it causes a violent headache and nausea, like a migraine, which can last for the rest of the day. I was sitting in front of the green and black computer screen for eight hours each weekday.

My manager introduced me to Access to Work - a government funded organisation committed to helping people with a disability to gain employment and stay in employment. They provided me with a large monitor and assessed my reading vision - this is where I discovered my preference for a simple font at 22 point.

The advisor described my sight as being like a cup of tea. Most people start the day with a full cup of sight, but mine is already half empty, so I only have useful sight for part of the day. It is important I rest my eyes as much as possible by closing them. If you speak to me on the telephone, I am likely to have my eyes closed. I did get some gentle teasing about appearing to be half asleep for most of the day, but it worked. I found there were very few activities where I needed to use my eyes. I was grateful to the teachers at Worcester for insisting I learnt to touch type. This advice was truly eye-opening (whoops!), and I still work this way in my own business today.

Excel spreadsheets are interesting with my nystagmus. Because of my constant eye movement, straight lines appear to move and undulate, and the cells appear to dance so I can't pin them down. Even when I enlarge the screen, I need to concentrate and work very slowly.

I have always suffered from dizziness. However, once I was working full time this became worse and I was diagnosed with positional vertigo also known as benign paroxysmal positional vertigo (BPPV). This causes intense dizziness and nausea when my head is in any position other than vertical, or when I turn quickly. It also happens frequently when travelling in a car or on an aeroplane.

I have always assumed this is linked to my nystagmus. However, despite many hours of research for this book, I have been unable to find any medical opinion which confirms nystagmus causes vertigo. In fact, the received opinion is vertigo causes nystagmus, rather than the other way round. Please let me know if you have any information on this.

A cure for my vertigo?

In order to be diagnosed with BPPV I had to undergo a series of very unpleasant tests. These included the *'tip test'* where I lay on a table which was tipped so my head was below my feet. After only a few seconds of this, the test had to be stopped due to my intense nausea.

The next test involved connecting electrodes to my head and spinning and tipping me in a chair. Again, this was very unpleasant. But the doctor had a problem with analysing the results. For most people, when they experience BPPV, this causes nystagmus. As I already have nystagmus, it was impossible for the tests to be interpreted in the usual way. I was also told for most nystagmus sufferers the eye movement decreases or even stops when they close their eyes. However, my eye movement increases when I close my eyes. I do like to be different!

I was given some medication to control the dizziness, but it was not effective, I quickly reverted to managing the condition on my own terms.

So, I will never be a Yoga master, or be able to bend down and find things under the sofa. I will never be comfortable on a roller coaster, but I have found ways to work with this discomfort in my working life.

Yes, I can use *"I will never..."* when describing activities I will never enjoy because of my disability.

At the time of writing this book, I am not aware of any research to lessen dizziness in nystagmus sufferers, nor have I encountered anyone else whose eye movement increases when they close their eyes.

As I have said, there are very few activities I can't do, but in this role, I learnt to problem solve to find my own way of doing things. Of course, I could write with my eyes closed if necessary!

Career progression

In my role of HR Assistant, I felt totally confident for the first time. In order to progress through the grades, I was very happy to be put through the same interview process as the other applicants, I soon progressed up two levels. I was no longer in a role that was ring-fenced for disabled applicants. I applied for the post of Senior HR Officer with Nottinghamshire County Council. There was only one position up for grabs, but both me and a colleague were successful. I was surprised, and I believed I was second choice but was given the role because of my visual impairment. I have no proof of this and didn't question it at the time, so I have no right to complain.

I was now involved in attendance management - working with managers to find a way forward for employees on sick leave. I would visit employees at home with their manager to discuss their options. Each Senior HR Officer would cover a geographical area, I was given Mansfield - which was the furthest area from my base at County Hall in West Bridgford! Normally, I would travel with a manager, but I also spent many hours in taxis.

I enjoyed the meetings at clients' homes from the start. There were the challenges of lighting and steps in each new environment, but I loved listening to every story, helping where I could. This experience would prove invaluable, ten years down the road, which I'll explain later in Chapter Eleven.

Some of these meetings were very tough. There were employees who were terminally ill, and my input was to discuss whether they would prefer to receive the immediate benefit of retirement on the grounds of ill health, or to die in service, in which case their family would receive the pay-out. I remember one visit in particular where the employee was only in her thirties and her two very small children were in the room. This was far tougher emotionally than any challenge I have faced in my own business. Experiences such as this made me forget about my own issues completely and be grateful for what I have.

Becoming a trainer

I trained as a trainer (another way of being the centre of attention) and gained more confidence to work in my own way. I didn't use coloured pens and would always nominate someone in the room to spot anyone with their hand up to ask a question. I ran training courses for managers on HR issues such as attendance management and recruitment.

In 1998, I became involved with the Springboard Programme, which was aimed at supporting female employees to progress up the ladder of their chosen career. I was trained to deliver their courses and of course I was the one who opted to deliver the training alone, rather than with a partner.

On one occasion, I trained a group of five women who were all older than me, on assertiveness, job application and interviews - it was so much fun. I would catch the bus to the training centre each day and walk to the venue - carrying all my training materials. I preferred to be independent, when possible, rather than asking for lifts.

From County Council to City Council

Five years on, I was successful at interview for a higher paid role as Senior HR Officer with Nottingham City Council. I would be managing a small team. This was ideal for me as it was based in the centre of Nottingham so easier to reach by public transport and the building was far more accessible. However, I swapped dark corridors for open plan offices, and had to learn where everyone sat. The Council eventually moved to hot-desking so my colleagues were in a different place each day. I would approach the person closest to me to ask them to give me directions to the person I was looking for. By now I was no longer embarrassed, just frustrated.

I was beginning to believe others would accept me as I am, and not consider me as unprofessional just because of my poor sight. Each time I rose up the career ladder, I was employed for decision-making, not form-filling or the dreaded filing.

My colleagues were incredibly supportive. There were six of us sharing an office, and most of the conversations were confidential. My screen was very large, so I always sat with my back to the wall so no one else could read it. I was often unaware of who was in the room, and the rest of the team developed a way of signalling to me if I needed to take my conversation elsewhere! Because I do not see or remember facial features well, I had to be especially careful I knew exactly who I was talking to. The admin staff took on a *'butler'* role announcing guests at a ball: *"John Smith - Head of Building Control to see you"* (m'lady!).

Reasonable adjustments

Thankfully employment legislation and Local Authority rules in the UK have changed considerably since 1996. There are no longer roles ring-fenced for disabled applicants, this was abolished by the Disability Discrimination Act 1995 and amended by the Equality Act 2010. Employers now have a duty to make *'reasonable adjustments'* for disabled staff. The Equality Act 2010 states, *'Your employer has a duty to take steps to remove, reduce or prevent the obstacles you face as a disabled worker or job applicant, where it is reasonable to do so.'*

Ironically, I was working in Human Resources at the time these changes came into force. My specialism was attendance management. I worked with employees to enable them to return to work following illness or injury, which may have caused them to fall under the legal definition of disability.

Often a reasonable adjustment is as simple as a new office chair, or a larger screen, but I remember working with a young man who had recently suffered an accident and was now confined to a wheelchair. As well as his new physical limitations, he was struggling with the emotion of his new way of life. It was very rewarding to help his manager to make changes to his role and surroundings to enable him to return to a full-time job.

Eye surgery?

I was soon studying again, this time for my Chartered Institute of Personnel and Development (CIPD) Post Graduate Diploma. This tested my *'half cup of sight'* to the limit. Every Wednesday, I would work from 08:00 until

12:30 and then walk to the nearby university for the lectures which ran from 13:00 until 20:00. My weekends were spent on coursework. This was the first time in my life I relied on tablets for the eye-strain headaches. I was very relieved to pass first time and get my social life back.

When I was 29, my consultant mentioned at a routine eye check-up there was a possibility I could have some corrective surgery which would mean no more contact lenses. I might also gain some sight and might even... be able to drive! I didn't hear anything he said after that and made an appointment to see the consultant surgeon as soon as I possibly could.

When I arrived at my appointment, I was asked to take out my contact lenses, I had dilating drops put into my eyes, which blurred my vision even more and left me totally at the mercy of the clinic staff. I was led to a large black leather chair - like a dentist's chair but with more widgets. It was very comfortable, but I was quite worried about where my lens case was and how I would find the door afterwards. I noticed with alarm there was a metal hoop above my head, and I had a vision of this being used as a clamp. I was terrified already. I have watched too much science fiction in my life and my imagination ran wild.

The door opened and the Great Man entered the room. He was blurrily large and imposing with a bushy black beard and a turban. He did not introduce himself to me. He was followed by several acolytes in white coats. The Great Man walked across to my chair and the others stood in a loose semi-circle facing me. Everything was blurred, but I guessed there were about eight of them. Nobody spoke to me. The Great Man asked each of his students to examine me and give him their findings. One by one they stepped forward and used lights and lenses to examine my eyes. The only time they spoke was to give me commands, *"Look up"*, or *"Blink"*. There were no "Please" or "Thank you" and no warning when my eyelid was about to be lifted.

Finally, the Great Man himself stepped forward. He made a short examination and then asked his students to give their opinion. I was pleased to note they had spotted the nystagmus, and also my pale and thin optic nerve, but there was a feeling of excitement in the room that unnerved me. They were suggesting treatments they had no experience of on a patient with my eye conditions. The Great Man was excited too and finally he spoke to me. He said he had never operated on a patient with nystagmus but would be willing to operate on me to potentially slow down my eye movement and give me better vision. If I had my lenses in, I would have run from the room. But instead, I calmly stated, "I will think about it", I made my escape as quickly as I could, and ignored the follow up letters.

I would love to have more sight, but I don't want to be a guinea pig!

Be careful what you wish for!

The last leg

My manager was the Departmental Head of HR, and when she took some time off, myself and a colleague covered for her. Then, in 2006, I had the chance to apply for the role of Head of HR for another department. After two days of interviews, I got the job.

The Grand Office

One of my favourite films is *Working Girl* with *Melanie Griffith, Sigourney Weaver* and *Harrison Ford*. If you have seen it, you will remember the scene where *Tess (Melanie Griffith)* gets her dream job in a large office with plate glass windows and a stunning view over Statton Island. She puts her feet up on the desk and rings her best friend with the words, *"Guess where I am?"*.

This is how I felt in as I walked into my new office on a cold winter's day at the start of a New Year, as Head of HR for Neighbourhood Services for Nottingham City Council. It had a stunning view of... the incinerator chimney and the bin lorries rolling by. Due to its proximity to the rubbish incinerator, the office also had blue fly traps on the walls which buzzed every few minutes as another bluebottle met its end.

But the office had (drum roll please):

A very large desk with my own PC and printer,

A conference table large enough to seat eight people,

AND

A three-seater sofa.

I giggled as I moved round the room, sitting on each seat in turn. There was a window into the main office, through which I could see my team of around 40 people working away. I rang my mum, and then my best friend and told them both how happy I was.

My days consisted of committee meetings and summons from senior managers. I dealt with disciplinary, grievance appeals and redundancies. Every process was adversarial, with a winner and a loser; I wasn't helping anyone. I no longer visited employees at home, and my role was strategic and *'political'* which is just not me!

But this is what I had worked for all of my life.

I had made it, I had climbed to my (professional) summit!

I had proved the doubters wrong and,

I HATED the job!

It took me several months to admit to myself my dream job was one which was not right for me!

How can I help YOU

I have an extensive knowledge of employment law, both from my 20 years working in Human Resources, and my status as a disabled employee. I work with organisations to bring my own brand of diversity awareness to senior managers and employees.

Chapter Nine
Rainbow After The Storm

*Disability doesn't make you exceptional
but questioning what you think
you know about it does.*
Stella Young

Until my mid-30s I believed everything that happened in my life, good or bad, was because of my disability. Then life came and hit me in the face.

Now, I must share the darkest years of my life so far. Most of what happened in these years is not related to my sight issues, but my differences made some of the decisions harder for me than they may have been for a fully sighted person.

In 2002, Martyn and I started trying for a baby. I knew that there were some friends who thought this was a bad idea, but we had been together for fifteen years and we felt that we were a strong enough team to cope. I was in my thirties and my biological clock was very loud.

We consulted a geneticist, who confirmed there was a 50% chance of Martyn passing on his glaucoma. I had a brain scan and was told it was highly unlikely I would pass on

FAQ

Are there any positives about your disability?

As I don't drive, I don't have to worry about how much I drink.

I will never have the expense or hassle of running a car.

I have been known to use my symbol cane to get to the front of a concert or cinema audience.

I still have an *'off switch'*. When I take my contact lenses out at night, I generally fall asleep very quickly.

My eyes can make anything into art. What you see as a dreary urban landscape, I can see as a beautiful painting, as I see just the shapes and colours, without the nuances of meaning.

But most of all, if I had full sight, I wouldn't be me!

my eye conditions to a child. We were excited about the prospect of becoming parents.

But after three years of trying, seeking medical advice and of me taking medication, nothing had happened. I was told I had Polycystic Ovary Syndrome (PCOS), and this would make it difficult to conceive.

In Vitro Fertilisation (IVF)

In early 2005, we went for a consultation about private IVF treatment. We did some tests and awaited the results eagerly.

I had been working for Nottingham City Council for four years at this point and enjoying my job. However, one morning in February 2005, a colleague came and asked me a question about apprenticeships. It was the sort of question I was asked regularly, but for no apparent reason I couldn't get my thoughts together and instead burst into tears.

I didn't know what was wrong. My colleagues were concerned about me, I was sent home (where I cried at old films and ate chocolate all day). It took me a few days to realise what might be wrong and on the 28th February 2005 I found out I was pregnant! We were both so excited and told everyone (not the done thing I know).

A few days later we received confirmation from the IVF clinic - they would not consider us for treatment because of our eye conditions. I tore up the letter - we didn't need them! I am not sure whether the criteria for IVF have now changed, I gave no more thought to this decision.

First pregnancy

I didn't feel too bad over the next few weeks, and on 4th May we went together for a routine midwife appointment. I remember the whole day in detail. On our short walk to the doctor's surgery, we were giggling together about it being *Star Wars Day* (the first time I had heard this phrase), but our mood soon changed. The midwife could not find our baby's heartbeat. She reassured us there was probably nothing to worry about but to get the baby moving suggested, *"Go and eat some chocolate and jump up and down a bit"*. But when we went back, there was still no sign of the baby. We travelled to the hospital on the bus and waited anxiously for an ultrasound scan.

There are times when I wish my sight was worse than it is. I can never forget the image on the screen of my baby just floating there with no movement and no heartbeat. Two doctors were called and pronounced him dead at sixteen weeks gestation. Words cannot describe how we felt. Martyn had a nose-bleed, and we were taken into the family room to discuss *'the next steps'*. I was given a tablet to start the birth process and told to come back three days later.

We were numb. We made the journey home on the bus, neither of us thought to phone a friend or a taxi. We cried together and rang my mum, who came up from Salisbury to be with us.

The next few days were indescribably sad. I still had my baby bump, but I knew the baby was dead. I blamed myself - even though I hadn't done anything to put the baby in danger. Friends and colleagues arrived with flowers and didn't know what to say. In the evenings, we sat and blindly looked at the television.

On 8th May, I went back to the hospital and gave birth to our little boy. He was tiny and his facial features were not fully formed, but he was our son. We had a few minutes with him and were told there would need to be an investigation into why he had died. This showed he had a hole in his heart, and if he had lived to full-term, he would have had severe challenges - but this was no consolation. We could not bear to give him a name.

We had previously worried about passing on our sight problems, but now we had to consider a heart condition as well.

I struggled back to work after a few weeks, but my manager was pregnant, and it was a difficult time for me.

A second loss

In November 2005, I found out I was pregnant again. I had weekly tests because of my history but lost the baby at five weeks gestation. I was not sure I could face another loss and was soon back at work.

It was at this point I was promoted to Departmental Head of HR. The role I craved and hated in equal measure. The office was large, but the timing was lousy.

In June 2006, Martyn and I went on holiday to Tenerife, to a hotel we had been to several times before where we met up with friends. While we were there it became obvious that Martyn's sight was deteriorating, and I needed to guide him around. It was very frightening for both of us. On our first day home, I went with him to the eye clinic at the hospital and he was told it was likely he would soon lose his sight altogether.

Even though we had always known this could happen, it felt as if the world was ending. Martyn was taken straight to a ward and put on a drip, but his sight was getting worse each day. I remember standing at the foot of his bed and making him tell me what colour top I was wearing to make sure he could still see me. I was devastated on the first day he couldn't give me an answer.

While sitting at the side of Martyn's bed one day I started to feel ill. A test confirmed I was pregnant again. I was scared - the timing could not be worse. How would we cope?

Martyn was in hospital for a few days and had eye surgery, but we were told it was too late to save his sight. I waited until he was home to tell him about the baby. After four years of wanting to be parents, we had to have a conversation about whether we should end the pregnancy. Thank goodness we made the right decision.

The summer of 2006 was *'interesting'* to say the least. Martyn was signed off work following his eye surgery and I was off work with horrendous morning sickness. We sat and watched the cricket together - it felt surreal.

I had regular tests, the baby seemed to be doing well, but we were both worried about losing another one, and we didn't make any preparations. Martyn's managers at the County Council were very supportive and he was soon back at work with some assistive technology and a support worker.

I went back to work too, but it was hard. I wanted to do as little as possible to concentrate on keeping our baby safe.

An anxious few months

The baby was due in March 2007, but I was signed off work in January following a bleed.

One month later, in the early hours of 9th February 2007 I woke thinking my waters had broken but it was blood. I will never forget the look on the faces of the paramedics at the amount of blood in my bedroom, and the thought of carrying a 9 month pregnant woman down the stairs. But in the end, I walked to the ambulance. I remember the paramedic saying to us, *"You know what this means don't you".* We could only nod mutely at him. They couldn't find a heartbeat. At 03:00 I was wheeled to the maternity ward with Martyn holding onto the foot of the trolley as the only means of guiding him.

We were taken to a private room, and I had a baby heart monitor strapped to my stomach. There it was - a good strong heartbeat! Our baby was determined to survive against the odds. I was advised to stay in hospital until he was born.

We couldn't have managed the next few weeks without my parents. They drove Martyn to and from the hospital every evening after work. He brought me a meal on Valentine's Day, making the other ladies jealous.

Most of the girls on the ward were younger than me. They would come in for a couple of days, have their babies and go home. I became a fixture - my whole day revolving around the food trolley at 12:00 and 17:00! It doesn't take long to become institutionalised.

I had a private room, which was easier for Martyn and me to navigate than a large ward. I had a TV and a private bathroom and didn't feel ill, so it was not too bad. The baby heart monitor was strapped to me twice a day. Sometimes it took a while for them to find him. The midwives would tell me, *"He is definitely a boy - he wriggles out of the way"* but he was always there. He was doing fine.

I was still scared. We had been through so much. Even if he was OK, how would we cope? We had been a team for twenty years, supporting each other with our differing levels of sight. By now, Martyn was completely blind and would never see our baby.

Every mother has a birth story. Mine involved 48 hours with no pain relief followed by an emergency Caesarean Section. Martyn wanted to be with me for this, which meant my mum was there as well to be his guide.

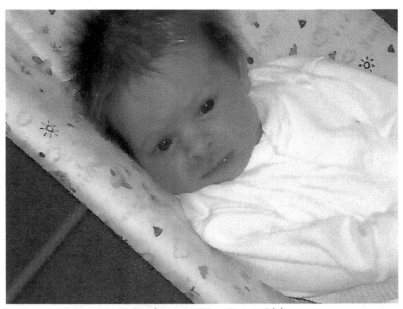

Matthew at Five Days Old

Welcome Matthew David Harris

Our son Matthew David Harris was born on 28th February 2007 (two years to the day since I found out I was pregnant for the first time). He needed oxygen at first but was soon asleep in an incubator at my side. He was beautiful.

I was in hospital for five days after the birth. As I was confined to bed, the midwives taught Martyn to change a nappy by touch. They would load the changing trolley in exactly the same way for him each day, he was soon handling nappies like a pro. I immediately loved being a mum. Martyn and I started to deal with the challenges of parenthood with sight loss one day at a time.

Our Family of Three

Our Family of Three

Martyn was a fantastic dad from the start. He was very hands on - changing nappies and feeding the baby regularly. The only real difference from fully sighted parents was I couldn't let Matthew fall asleep on his quilt on the floor when Martyn was in the house, and I had to choose a bus-friendly pram - as do many parents. We also opted for ready-made milk rather than measuring out the powder (as usual the more expensive option).

Matthew Asleep on the Quilt

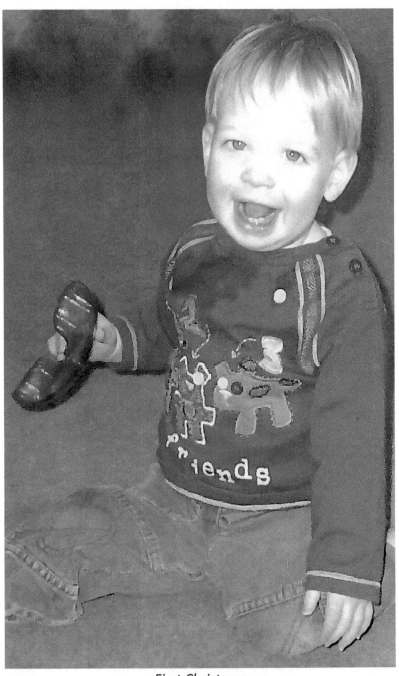

First Christmas

I am not religious but during these two years I began to believe things happen for a reason. The world had decided Martyn would have to lose his sight before we could have a child.

So, in April 2007, I was on maternity leave from a job I hated whilst coming to terms with Martyn's blindness. Due to my miscarriages I had a fear we would somehow lose Matthew, too. This on top of the sleepless nights made me reach a really low point in my life.

Of course, Martyn was facing his own challenges. His useful sight was gone, and he had to find innovative new ways to do the simplest everyday tasks.

Work decisions

I had a call from my manager asking me to come to a meeting. I hadn't left the baby with anyone yet. I didn't want to think about work at all and I resented this interruption to family life. But I was told the meeting was very important. I left Matthew with mum and dad (they were very excited!) and went into work.

The reason for the meeting was my department of the Council was being closed with all the teams merged into other departments. Instead of making me redundant, we were told all the Heads of HR could apply for the reduced number of posts. This would need to happen before the end of my maternity leave. I did not relish the thought of a recruitment process for a job I did not enjoy. Just two days later, I contacted my manager and offered to take a demotion to Senior HR Officer, which meant I could work more flexible hours, and my colleagues would not need to go through the recruitment process. It was not a difficult decision to make - my priorities had changed. I wanted to put my family above my career.

The next two years were the best of my HR career. I worked on attendance management in a small and friendly HR team. I managed two of the HR officers, which I enjoyed. I made long term friends.

Then, in 2010, came another change. The Council were moving all the HR teams into a large building with open plan floors. We would all be hot-desking, booking a different desk each day. This would clearly be challenging for me with my large screen, I worked again with *Access to Work* to set up a desk to suit me, so I didn't need to move around. The lighting was dim at best, and I struggled to find people in the office, as they all moved around each day. I had some very high-profile disciplinary cases to manage, which involved senior managers, but my *'half-cup of sight'* was being used up at home.

All the internal walls in the new office were glass and I often bumped into them. They all had *'visibility stickers'* to avoid this, but with my eye movement, I didn't see these.

In late 2010, there was another restructure of the HR team planned, again we would all have to re-apply for our jobs. This time redeployment was not an option as the whole of HR were in the same building, which I was finding difficult to navigate.

We were all given the option of voluntary redundancy. I very much wanted to leave, I would receive a good pay-out, but was very anxious about what I could do next. I had only ever worked in the public sector, where there was generally good provision for employees with disabilities.

I may never work again. Matthew was due to start school in a few months and I needed the flexibility to spend quality time with him.

My whole life had been about my career until this point. At the age of 40, I had absolutely no idea what would come next.

Martyn

Chapter Ten
Into The Darkness

To be blind is not miserable;
not to be able to bear blindness,
that is miserable.

John Milton

Although we were both aware Martyn could go blind, neither of us were prepared for just how quickly it would happen.

The day the lights went out

At the fateful eye appointment in July 2006, Martyn's eye pressure, in his one useful eye, was up at 40 - a safe level is below 15. He should have been experiencing glaucoma headaches, the consultant saw it as a bad sign he had no pain. It showed some nerves around his eye had died. Martyn's right eye, which has been blind since the age of seven, is soft to the touch and has a pressure around four.

Martyn had to be admitted to hospital immediately, to try and save his sight. While the consultant left the room to make these arrangements, I remember the two of us crying together - we both knew what this meant.

Martyn's point of view

I am blind. Please don't use any other word. I have no sight at all. I am not aware of a hand waving in front of my face, or a bright light shining in my eyes - there is nothing.

Both of my optic nerves have now died, so both eyes are losing all colour and appear sunken into my head (so Amanda tells me).

I know this is how I will be for the rest of my life. There is no point in me being upset about this, so I get on with life. However, I do get frustrated about the activities I can't do - most accessible computer games are boring, and I rely on good radio commentary for the football and cricket.

But most of my frustration comes from the actions and perceptions of other people. For example:

> Yes, I do have a full-time job. I am employed for my decision-making ability, which is not affected by my blindness.

> I do not live in a residential care home. I am lucky enough to live in a house with my family.

> When I am outside, I wear dark glasses - this is not to protect my eyes from glare - which I can't see. Rather this is to protect my eyes from stray branches sticking out over the pavement, and from the weather as my eyes can become very dry.

I don't read Braille to a high standard. I know basic Braille with just enough to play cards with the family. As I lost my sight in my thirties, it was very late to learn, and I do not have good sensitivity in my fingertips - probably from all the hands-on cooking I have done. As famous chef *Marco Pierre White* says, *"Fingers are for burning"*.

My lifeline is my IPhone with the voiceover function. It allows me to dictate shopping lists, and has an application (app) to recognise colours, and barcodes. I can also use it as a walking satnav. The 21st Century is a good time to be blind (if that is possible) as life is easier than ever with modern technology. I have speech software on my computer, and we have several smart speakers in the house.

I don't have a guide dog - I use a long cane.

My biggest pet hate at work is when colleagues send me documents with track changes in red.

If you have any other questions, please ask.

Later that day, Martyn had his third trabeculectomy operation, followed by a laser surgery and was on a fluid drip - but it was too late, his sight was fading rapidly. I remember the day when he could not tell me what colour I was wearing.

We all have so many preconceptions about what it means to be blind, what blind people can and can't do. Martyn has achieved so much since he lost his sight and had exceeded everybody's expectations - except his own. He set himself high standards and has kept to them. Since that day in the consultant's office, I have only seen him upset once, but I am aware of his frustrations.

On leaving hospital, he took two weeks off work, during which time his manager arranged for him to have a support worker on his return. He still tells people that he has never had a day off sick from work, *"Except the two weeks after I lost my sight"*. Initially, he was prescribed a pair of glasses which enhanced his vision a little - just to indistinct shapes and colours, but within a few months, he was totally blind.

He bought a long mobility cane - one that reaches the ground and has a ball on the end for feeling his way around. Of course, he had to relearn his way to work and did the dreaded mobility training. Walking along a pavement is relatively easy as he can feel the curb, but his nemesis is large open spaces like the one at the front of his office.

At first, he would walk round the edge of the space, but has now adjusted to the exact angle to get to the front door. By the way, mobility canes are relatively expensive, and he always needs a spare as he cannot go out without one. Canes usually end up broken either under the wheels of a car or bus, or just through constant daily use. Just another regular item of expenditure in our house.

Martyn soon learned not to bump into walls or furniture in the house, but he still needs to concentrate even in familiar surroundings, as he is reliant on his memory, not his cane.

I went with him to work for the first few days, walking behind him so he was effectively on his own. I will never forget my sheer dread the first time I watched him cross a road on his own with no sight. Almost fifteen years later I still don't know how he does this safely using just hearing. He likes to stick his white cane out into the road, so any approaching traffic has no choice but to stop.

All the local bus drivers know him and will wait for him at the bus stop if they can see him approaching. He is particularly friendly with the female bus drivers for some reason - he still has his boyish charm.

After losing his sight, Martyn returned to work full time in his previous role of Team Leader. He managed a team of ten people in an open plan office, he would walk round the office and speak to each team member at the start of the day. He has the admiration and respect of all of his colleagues, I am in awe of his courage and persistence.

Guide dog

Martyn was doing well with his white cane but walking with a cane is a slow process and he often came home with grazes on his forehead from a *'stray'* lamppost. So, after two years of blindness, he applied to have a guide dog.

Each guide dog is specifically matched to their prospective owner and that often means a long wait for the right dog. Within a few weeks of his application, we welcomed into our family a beautiful chocolate Labrador called Marcie.

Before Martyn could bring Marcie home, he spent two weeks at a local hotel with her, for them to bond, to get used to each other. Matthew, our son, was two years old, and we were only allowed to visit Martyn once during training. This was difficult for Matthew to accept at such a young age.

Guide dogs are working dogs, not pets, and we were advised to treat Marcie accordingly. We were instructed that only Martyn could give her fuss and feed her. You can imagine how difficult this was for Matthew and me. Matthew loved to pet her and let her lick his hands. Our two cats were not so keen on the new arrival!

Martyn and Marcie

138

Like all dogs, Marcie enjoyed eye contact with humans, which Martyn could not give to her. It was therefore important that she did not get this from the rest of the family, as she needed to stay bonded with Martyn. If you meet a guide dog in the street, do not bend down to give them some fuss and eye contact. Remember, they are working dogs, not pets.

A guide dog is just a very well-trained dog. This may seem obvious, but to watch many working guide dogs with their owners, you would think they understand English. Martyn and Marcie worked with a support worker from Guide Dogs UK to learn the route to work via bus, and to the shops. Martyn could now walk at speed and would regularly walk the three miles to work with Marcie to give her some exercise. Of course, she also had a run off the harness whenever possible.

I must stress the events I am about to share are extremely rare. Guide Dogs UK is an amazing organisation and having experienced the difference a dog can make to a blind person's life I have no hesitation in recommending them.

However, within a few months of meeting Marcie, things started to go wrong. At work, Martyn had a special place to take her to *'spend'*. This was concreted and enclosed so that Martyn could find the excrement and pick it up. He took her down there several times during each working day.

Marcie had been trained to sit when she reached a curb - Martyn was in charge of deciding when it was safe to cross the road. Unfortunately, Marcie started to leave poo on curbs, and there were a couple of incidents when she urinated in Martyn's office. This should not have happened.

Then one day when Martyn was crossing a dual carriageway outside his office, Marcie did not guide him to the central reservation, but instead walked halfway across the road and sat down. With cars whizzing past on both sides, and not knowing whether the far pavement was straight ahead, Martyn was disorientated and helpless. Luckily a driver stopped and helped him to the other side of the road.

But Martyn had then lost his trust in Marcie. He contacted Guide Dogs UK, who realised that Marcie had failed her training. We had to let her go. All three of us were distraught. Imagine giving up your dog after a year of

Danger with a Guide Dog

sharing your home with her. Matthew didn't understand, we couldn't tell him Marcie was leaving because she had been naughty - he might have worried he would be next.

Since then, Martyn has not felt able to have another guide dog. Maybe in the future he will change his mind. As I write, Martyn is working from home following the COVID pandemic, so it is perhaps as well that he does not currently have a dog.

Onwards and upwards

When Matthew started at the local primary school, Martyn learned the route to the school and would sometimes take him or bring him home. He would not go into the playground - a wide open space full of noise and small children who he could knock over, so from an early age, Matthew learned to meet his dad at the school gate. There are no roads to cross on this route, and Matthew was starting to learn about guiding, but he did once deliberately walk his dad into a lamppost. All children push the boundaries, but maybe he was also testing whether his dad would have any awareness of the danger ahead.

Martyn soon joined the governing body at the school, and within a couple of years he was Chair of Governors. He continues to enjoy this role today, despite Matthew having moved on to secondary school.

At the same time, he became Chair of the Association of Public Authority Deputies (APAD). This is a national organisation representing all Local Authorities in the UK, he travelled nationwide to meetings for several years, with his support worker.

Support worker

The role of support worker for a blind person is an unusual one. His workers need to have physical contact with him, as he holds an elbow to be guided. They also need to be pragmatic if he accidentally touches them in an inappropriate place. All his support workers to date have been female, all have learned that there are times where the best course of action is to physically lead Martyn by both arms to take him away from danger.

I still guide Martyn by holding his hand, but Matthew has learnt to guide by elbow - no teenager wants to be seen holding their dad's hand in public.

Martyn's skills and interests

After ten years in Adult Client Finance, Martyn took a sideways move to work in Commissioning for the County Council. He no longer manages a team, but he works closely with local NHS services on funding issues and deputises at meetings for senior managers. He really enjoys his job - I have no idea why - it is endless meetings, writing reports and procedures - each to their own, I guess.

Martyn enjoys listening to the *'mighty'* Manchester United and cricket commentary on the radio, and audio books. He has a large collection of headphones, and always buys new models as they are released. Any misunderstandings in our family are usually because I can't see he has his headphones on, and he can't hear me talking to him.

Martyn loves to cook, using smell and touch to ensure food is cooked properly. I, on the other hand, get out the magnifying glass to read the cooking instructions (why are they always too small). I need to cook by numbers.

At the age of 35, Martyn began a course in Braille. There are two grades of Braille - level one includes all of the letters of the alphabet, but this can be slow to read. Level two uses *'contractions'*, which are often one symbol to represent a common letter combination, a word or phrase. Braille users read with both hands - one in front of the other - to increase their speed. As with most skills, reading Braille is easier to master when you are young. Not only was Martyn in his thirties by this point, but after all those years of turning the steak in the pan with his bare hands, he had lost a lot of the sensitivity in his finger ends. Nowadays, he knows enough Braille to play cards with an adapted pack, but for most tasks he uses talking apps.

Martyn has taught me how to use humour to overcome challenges. He once told his eye consultant that he could see better after a few glasses of gin and asked if there was any chance of a research grant to prove this! When we are watching television, we will argue about what the actors look like. He *'sees'* all female characters as brunettes. However, the last time he saw me, I was 35 years old, and he can remember what I looked like at 17 years, but has not seen me at 50, which has its advantages.

We were together for twenty years before we had Matthew, and we learned to work and play as a team. It is easy now to forget that Martyn's sight has never been perfect, I tend to divide our lives together into two distinct eras - before and after Martyn's blindness. But he faced challenges even when he had some useful sight.

Martyn's pragmatic belief is that his sight cannot get any worse, he is otherwise fit and healthy. As always, I am less practical and more emotional about our situation.

Amanda with Grandpa

Chapter Eleven
Finding My Passion

*Find summat you enjoy doing, then find
some eejit who'll pay you to do it.*

**Frederick Lewis Beeken
(My wonderful Yorkshire Grandpa)**

At the age of 40, I finally followed my grandpa's advice from 30 years earlier. I now had the confidence to make the most of my abilities.

In December 2010, I pressed the *'Send'* button on the email asking for voluntary redundancy from the City Council, and within a week it was approved - I had an end date of 1st April 2011. After more than fifteen years of employment in Nottinghamshire County Council and Nottingham City Council, I was walking away. It felt like the right thing to do but it was a very anxious time.

The thoughts keeping me awake at night were:

Had I just given up on eating out, holidays and all the other things we enjoy as a family?

What would I do?

FAQ
How can I help?

I never refuse a well meant and useful offer of help. But I prefer to let you know when I need help. I have had to learn to trust myself. I am the expert in my own visual impairment, and I have learned to challenge myself to do things others may suggest I can't do.

Is there a difference between *'fiercely independent'* and *'stubborn'*? My friends would probably say not. As I get older, I find it easier to ask for help, but I struggle not to be blunt if help is offered when I don't need it. I imagine this is a contradiction faced by many disabled people. I would prefer to do things myself when I can.

However, I can enjoy activities where I need some help. I love to dance, but often need to be guided through the crowd to the dance floor.

Please be aware of the difference between, *"How can I help?"* which is always acceptable, and, *"Here, let me help"* (usually said while taking over the task). Just because I am holding something close to my face and have one eye shut, does not mean I am struggling. This is normal for me, and I will not be aware of how it looks.

Would I ever get another job? (As a visually impaired 40 year old this may be difficult.)

If I started my own business, I would have to do things differently from other people.

Would clients accept me? Or would they consider me slow and unprofessional?

What if I never worked again?

Would I get eyestrain from all the reading?

I remember I was sitting at our dining table writing Christmas cards when Martyn made the suggestion which would change my life. He had experience of Lasting Powers of Attorney through his role with the Council, and suggested people would pay me to create and register these for them.

I didn't really know what Lasting Powers of Attorney meant, so I turned to trusty Google for advice. I discovered there were independent Will Writers who worked from home and visited clients to take instructions for Wills and Lasting Powers of Attorney.

But surely, I couldn't do that? I can't drive. I need large print and good light to do anything. I knew nothing about running my own business.

Self-employment - a leap in the dark

Despite many misgivings, I found myself considering Martyn's suggestion as a serious option. After a few weeks, I contacted the Society of Will Writers and booked myself on an introductory course.

I also sourced some free advice about running my own business. In preparation for a meeting with my business

Receiving my First Cheque

advisor, I wrote a long list of tasks I thought I would need to do before I could ask people to pay me to write their Wills.

When I arrived at the meeting, I unfolded my list - one sheet of A4 filled front and back with bullet points. The advisor smiled. Instead of going through my list, he asked me to talk about my concerns. I told him about my fears that my visual impairment would be too much of a barrier.

I owe this advisor a lot. He gently persuaded me to tear up my list and just do four things:

Do the training with the Society of Will Writers.

Open a business bank account.

Arrange the relevant business insurance, and then

Advertise my service to test whether it was viable.

He said everything else on the list could wait.

My first client

I met my first client at a business start-up course. He wanted me to produce a Lasting Power of Attorney for his mum. I was so nervous. He was happy to be my guinea pig and I learnt as I went along. I was lucky - the address was in Nottingham city centre, so I went by bus. I found I felt confident sitting in someone's home and taking instructions - it was very similar to the attendance management visits I had done with the Council. I pulled on my past experience, ever grateful for this part of my life, and my sight was not an issue.

A week later my new client handed me a cheque - I had actually earned money, and this was the start of my love for being self-employed. I met a friend for lunch afterwards and I remember grinning foolishly and waving the cheque at her. I had the thought that I might frame it, but she sensibly told me it would be more use in the bank!

Finding my clients (literally)

Martyn worked with a financial advisor, who offered to refer some of his clients to me. I admired his trust at this point. Within a few days, I answered my phone to my first *'stranger'* client. We arranged the appointment in my (empty) diary, and he told me he lived in Cotgrave.

I wasn't sure where Cotgrave was, let alone how I would get there. I knew my mum would drive me if I asked her - but that was no way to run a business! I needed to prove (to myself) I could do this on my own. (Have I mentioned I can be stubborn?). So, I looked on the *Travelwise* website and planned the bus journey. It would be two buses, I had plenty of time to travel there, but I had many questions:

> How would I find the house?
>
> Could I read house numbers? (I had never turned up at someone's house before - not even the house of a friend - I had always been chaperoned.)
>
> Would I look stupid squinting at houses?
>
> Would I be arrested for loitering?

Thankfully, *Google Earth* came to my rescue. I found I could walk from the bus stop to my client's house virtually, and even work out house numbers, before making the journey. This was very time-consuming, and I was still anxious as I set off on the day. I had written out the names of all the bus stops, so I knew when my stop was coming - but I found to my amazement there were audio announcements on the bus for each stop so I wouldn't need this.

Once off the bus, I soon learned Google Earth is not ideal preparation for a journey. It does not help with the crossing of busy roads, or where there is no footpath on a stretch of road. If I had thought about this before, I would have been more anxious - but I found I just dealt with the obstacles one at a time. I even felt confident enough to walk up some driveways to get close enough to read house numbers.

I was half an hour early and ended up hanging around in the street until it was time to go in. I don't remember the meeting - I had spent so much time preparing for the journey, that the interview with the client was almost secondary and again felt very natural.

I was soon visiting two or three clients in a week - never more than one a day - so the bus worked well. I stopped using Google Earth and learned to trust myself to read road signs and house numbers. I was now working out for myself how much useful sight I have.

One journey to a client in my first few weeks stands out. I am standing on an unfamiliar street in the dark. It is raining and my *'helpful'* brain tells me the reflections of the streetlamps in the puddles are actually lights on the ground that I should avoid, and there are no steps at the kerb edge - experience tells me there are steps and I have to feel for them with my foot. I ignore the signals from my brain and look for house numbers. The drives are long, and I walk up one of them to get close enough to see a house number. I then return to the pavement and count the houses until

I find what I think is the right one. This is no mean feat as the houses are a mixture of detached and semis with lights in windows and doors which move around in the dark as I look at them. I believe I have identified the correct house.

My target house has a huge white van parked between the gateposts - so close on both sides that I can't get past it. This is the sort of situation that has been running through my head at 03:00 and making me anxious. Suddenly, my attitude changes from anxiety to determination.

I knock at the door of the nearest house. A lady opens the door a crack - keeping it on the chain. I guess she doesn't trust anyone who is out in this weather. She confirms her neighbour is the house I am looking for and then she slams the door.

My only option now is to ring my client. The phone number is on the papers in my briefcase. I squat on the pavement and pull out the papers, and my phone, shielding them from the rain. I get out my reading glasses and a magnifying glass to read the phone number. I dial apprehensively:

Client: Hello. (The voice is friendly)

Me: Hello, this is Amanda Harris, the Will Writer. I am at your house, but I can't get to your door because of the van on the drive. I am really sorry.

(My heart is racing - I must seem so stupid. There is a pause at the other end of the line. What is she thinking?)

Client: I will come and get you.

When my client approaches me, it is not from the drive with the van, but from a pedestrian path at the side of the house, which I haven't seen of course. My anxiety grows and

I feel the familiar hot and cold flashes of embarrassment.

But she is smiling, and I follow her up the path. When we get to the door, I remember to count the steps, as I will not be able to see them when I come out. We go inside and she hands me a towel.

She looks at me quizzically as she makes me a cup of tea. I will have to tell her about my visual impairment! Will she think I am stupid and unprofessional? I have no choice. I explain my disability and her smile returns. She is curious about how much I can see. She and her husband sit down and take my advice on their estate planning.

This was a revelation to me. At the time I thought it would not happen again. In ten years of running my business, whenever I explain my visual impairment to a client, they are understanding. If I need to wait for a taxi, I am offered another cup of tea. I have been given vegetables from allotments, and lifts home. I have brought bunches of flowers home on the bus, and on one memorable occasion I nearly came home with a pair of kittens!

When I left the client's house on that dark and rainy night, I discovered that I had almost an hour to wait for the next bus home. I needed to find a smarter way to travel.

'Access to Work'

I had already contacted Access to Work about my needs for my home office. They provided me with a large monitor and some additional training on keyboard shortcuts so I could avoid using the mouse too much (I often lose that pesky cursor!). I knew they would pay transport costs for workers with disabilities, so I submitted a claim.

The Access to Work advisor asked me where my office was - and what time each day I needed to travel from home to the office. I told her I needed to be able to travel to clients throughout Nottinghamshire at different times of the day, including evenings. There was a pause on the other end of the phone. This advisor is another person whose name I will never forget. Her answer was constructive. Although this had not been done before by the local Access to Work Team, she would look into it and get back to me.

A few weeks later, I had an agreement from Access to Work that they would pay for me to use a driver to get me to my clients - with a taxi account as a backup. Taxis are not ideal as they are expensive if I ask them to wait for me during my visit. I never know exactly how long I will be with a client, and if I ring for a taxi home, I may have a considerable wait. I was concerned that clients would not want me to linger in their homes after I had finished my business. Of course, I was wrong about this. In the few times this has happened I have merely been offered another cup of tea and had a chat.

Taxis alone would be less practical than drivers. I had no help with finding drivers and again had to work out the best way to do this. Access to Work pay an hourly rate, and I pay mileage costs, but it is not a full-time job.

My drivers
There are days where I need a lift in the morning, afternoon and evening, but other days when I don't go anywhere. My mum was my first driver, followed by friends. I used the local Skills Exchange and found many people willing to help. My drivers have included retired people, students, people on maternity leave - often with a baby in the back

for me to coo over, and my virtual assistant.

My drivers do far more for me than just drive. They locate house numbers for me and point out any obstacles on the way to the door. My sight is particularly bad at night, and after an evening visit, I often walk out of the client's home and before my eyes have started to adjust, I hear the start of a car engine and see headlights to let me know where my driver is. It is like having a magic car which starts when it sees me.

I also ask my drivers to witness Wills when needed. They can choose which driving jobs to take each week, so they know the location and whether I need them as witness before they take the job.

Most importantly my drivers are now good friends. If I could drive, I would spend an inordinate amount of time alone in my car. They are the closest people I have as work colleagues and I appreciate every single one of them, I couldn't run the business without them now. They all know it is fine if they want to leave my drivers list too - for instance, if they find other work or have a change in circumstances.

I have a dreadful memory for routes and landmarks, which is understandable as everything is so blurred. I can't remember which house I visited yesterday. My drivers get used to this.

From the start of my business, I loved it. It combines my curiosity about people, with my interest in the Law. In HR, I was dealing with disciplinary processes, grievances and attendance management where there was always a *'loser'* in the process. I now have an office wall full of '*thank you*' letters from clients, and with the bonus of gaining friendships.

First years of the business

As with any business, the first couple of years were hard and I had times where there was no work. I had always worked full time, and I had very few friends who I could meet during the day. I started to become bored and decided to take a part time job to fill the time (and help with finances). I started to work in an admin role for Nottingham City Homes, which was not ideal, as a large part of my day involved entering data from the vehicle logs of the drivers. As I am not good at reading handwriting, or at using Excel, this was difficult. The eye strain returned.

I decided I had to leave and went to the HR department to give in my notice. I left that meeting with a temporary part time job in HR, managing sickness absence! After only a few weeks, I remembered why I left HR in the first place, and this time I left '*being employed*' permanently so I could put all my effort into growing my business.

My print advertising was working well, and I approached more financial advisors to pass business to me. I was now confident enough to explain my visual impairment and they were not put off. Over ten years later, I receive most of my clients from financial advisors, or from word of mouth.

Memorable clients

I have worked with hundreds of clients over the years, each has their own needs and their own story. Some clients stick in my memory. I once helped a single parent to make provision in her Will for the differing needs of her three autistic sons. I visited a couple where the wife had just learned her husband had a son with another woman and they trusted me to make Wills to suit this new situation.

The most harrowing client interaction of all is when I am asked to make a Will for someone coming to the end of their life. I visit the local hospice regularly and can produce Wills in a single day where needed. I often get letters from the family when their loved one has passed, thanking me for my help at a difficult time.

I do receive some humorous requests. One lady wanted to bequeath a large picture to her son in her Will. The clause read, *"Please hang this over your mantelpiece for a year and think of me".* She told me, *"He hates that picture".* Of course, this request was not legally binding, but it is possible to have a bit of fun with a Will at times.

Sharing my challenges

I genuinely believe when I explain my challenges to clients, this vulnerability helps to build trust more quickly. After all, they are sharing very personal details with me, and they welcome my openness.

I choose whether to tell my clients I have poor sight. Some clients notice I have a driver and I will explain why. I can even make a joke of it. I will often liken it to having a chauffeur and say I must get my driver a hat and white gloves. One client asked me if I had lost my licence through drink driving and I found myself entering into the *'spirit'* of it and quipping my reputation must have preceded me. Those of you who know me will attest I can't take my drink and two glasses of anything alcoholic will cause me to fall over.

Although most of my clients are in Nottinghamshire and surrounding areas, I have made longer journeys. A couple of years ago, one of my financial advisors referred to me a client in Wakefield. I hadn't been back to the city since I left Wakefield Girls' High School 30 years ago, but this would be a chance to catch up with some old friends. I caught the train from Nottingham to Wakefield. There were not many recognisable landmarks on the way, but then everything had always been blurred and it had been a long time.

I stepped out of the train, expecting a very familiar platform. But I didn't recognise anything. Surely after seven years of passing through here every day I would remember something? I checked the signs - yes, I was at Wakefield station. Maybe this was a different platform to the one I was used to.

I walked from the platform to the concourse, still not recognising anything at all. I know I don't have a good visual memory, but this was ridiculous. I stepped outside - I could vividly remember the car park I had walked across every day to school, with its steps down to the small road below. I had once been pulled across this road by an over helpful stranger. But the car park was not there - instead there were pedestrianised areas and shops. I began to feel quite discombobulated!

I shared my confusion with my client when she arrived. She laughed and explained this was a new station, built on a different site, to replace the old one, which was not fully accessible. I was very relieved, but a tad disappointed too. I wanted to visit old haunts.

Specific challenges

Entering a client's home for the first time can still be a challenge for me. The lighting might be dim, and steps are sometimes not obvious. A client will point the way, I will often not see this and walk the wrong way anyway. A step I took confidently on the way in may floor me (literally) on the way out. But I have learned to see the funny side and the worst I have ever suffered is a grazed knee.

In recent years, one of my main challenges has been shrinking technology. I have always used a PC with a large screen and have never owned a laptop as the screen is too small and low for me. But nowadays there is an app for everything. Although I own a smartphone and a tablet, I often have to resort to reading glasses and magnifying glass to use apps. There are some that allow for magnification on the screen, but many do not. My stubborn streak has so far prevented me from turning on the speech software on my devices! I am a fast typist but when it comes to the keyboard on a phone, I have very poor hand-eye coordination and my friends put up stoically with my errors.

I use my PC and large screen for everything. This has never been a problem, until I started to write this book. I would love to sit and write in the park or in a coffee shop. Many of my best ideas come to me when I am out of my office, and it would be great to separate my Will Writing from my book writing - but I have no choice but to type while surrounded by client files. I have tried to dictate while I am out, but I find the act of typing much easier than dictation.

There is a belief that if one sense is impaired, the others become more refined to compensate. This may well be true (my son is very aware of my good hearing for example) but this doesn't mean a disabled person has to LIKE doing things a different way, or that it doesn't matter to them, or that they have got used to it. I have been told, *"You must be used to not being able to drive, so it won't bother you."*

This is simply not true. If I didn't know that other people could drive, then it would not be an issue. There is a temptation for me to live my life with little contact with others, as I can then live in my own social model and not be reminded of my differences.

I was out for lunch with a friend a few days ago. On the way home, she took a detour to pick up something for her business. In a car, it is easy, but I would need to use either buses or a driver to make a quick detour. This would take time and cost money (although not as much money as running a car I understand). My life has to be planned out, and I can't have the same spontaneity as a fully sighted person. My life experience is therefore limited.

Because I see less, I know less. This means I won't just *'spot'* a new restaurant or a new pair of shoes in a shop window. I tend to visit the same shops and restaurants where I know the lighting will be good and the staff helpful. This affects my life experiences.

I know there are visually impaired people who climb mountains and play professional sport. I find these people truly inspiring - not just because of their exploits, but because they dare to be open about what they want to achieve, and about asking for fully sighted help. Maybe I am stubborn, but I enjoy doing activities which I can achieve without help - in the same way you do, I assume.

I have drivers for work, but if there is a journey I can make alone on public transport, then I will do this. In good weather I will walk to clients, or catch the bus, rather than using my drivers. Of course, this is getting less realistic now I am so busy as it takes time. But just because I need help, doesn't mean that I like it - or that I am so used to it that it doesn't bother me.

When searching for a new leisure activity my first consideration is whether I can achieve it without help. Maybe this is wrong, stubborn, or shy of me and maybe this will change as I get older.

How can I help YOU?

I can provide talks, workshops and Q&A sessions at secondary schools about running your own business and overcoming challenges to self-employment.

Supportive Family

Chapter Twelve
A Family of Mixed Abilities

Always remember that you are absolutely unique.
Just like everyone else.
Margaret Mead

Let's go back to the time when we became a family of three. We brought Matthew home at five days old and faced the same challenges as any other first-time parents. My mum and dad had driven the three of us home from the hospital with Matthew buried in a snowsuit which was at least two sizes too big for him. We transferred him, fast asleep, to his Moses basket and placed him on the floor of the sitting room. Then, we sat on the sofa and looked at each other.

What should we do now?

What happens next?

We rang for a pizza.

I had not changed a nappy yet, and Martyn felt like an expert. On my first attempt he was quite critical. *"Rachel (the midwife) didn't teach me to do it that way."* I was worried about cleanliness, so Matthew was the cleanest baby in Nottingham.

FAQ
Will your eyesight change?

Not in essence. However, I am experiencing the normal changes of ageing. My reading vision is deteriorating, and this is a problem as I can't use reading glasses for long periods of time.

My sight still changes slightly from day to day, and throughout the day. I am almost completely night blind and can see very little on a very sunny day too, as the glare gives me the impression of *'white out'*. Sunglasses remove the glare but also decrease my useful sight.

My eye movement increases when I am tired or stressed, which affects my sight significantly. I was once told my eye movement increases when I tell a lie - look out for that if you meet me.

I am once again exploring the option of eye surgery, so I could function without my contact lenses but I would then lose the ability to take out my lenses to read.

Most babies enjoy a wriggle in a baby 'gym', but I was always aware Martyn could not see him on the floor, so I would build a pile of soft toys around the gym so Martyn would kick them first.

At the end of a tiring day when Martyn had been at work, the floor would be covered with toys and other baby paraphernalia. There were times when, instead of clearing up, I would use a brush to clear a path from the front door to a chair for Martyn. He couldn't see the mess, and I would deal with it tomorrow.

Martyn has exceptional hearing, and if the baby was making any noise at all, he could confidently walk over to him and pick him up.

One challenge was the babygro's with poppers. Matthew was often wrongly poppered as it is difficult to get them straight without sight.

These were all things we could laugh at. But I was very anxious about losing Matthew. I had lost two babies already and I firmly believed something would happen to him. I kept him at my side in his Moses basket at night until he grew too big for this at six weeks old. Once he was in his cot in his room, I would get up several times during the night to check on him. I remember ringing the health visitor in a panic one morning - Matthew had been asleep since 22:00 and it was now almost 10:00! Yes, he was breathing and wasn't in distress. She laughed at me gently and advised me to make the most of it and go back to bed.

I was also convinced Social Services would class us as unfit parents, because of our disabilities. After all, we had been turned down for IVF before Martyn lost his sight. I worried

Matthew at One Month Old with his Dad

if we made one mistake then our beautiful son would be taken into care. Just before a regular medical check at about six weeks old, I noticed a bruise on Matthew's arm. I went into a panic. I thought of covering it with a plaster or bandage, but wouldn't this make it worse? Of course, the nurse saw the bruise. I started to stammer I didn't know what had caused it and I was really sorry. She was very reassuring - all babies get bumps and bruises sometimes and she had seen it all before. She was not concerned.

As a new parent, if a baby is ill, you are told to look out for a viral rash, and to press it with a glass to check for meningitis. I learned from experience I couldn't see a skin rash, but my mum was happy to come over and look at her grandson as often as possible.

At birth Matthew was a 'floppy baby' and had been diagnosed with Joint Hypermobility syndrome. Over his first year we were told:

He may never feed properly.

He may struggle to sit and even,

He may never walk.

Luckily, he has the same attitude as me, and although he was late to crawl and walk, he got there in the end. Eating has never been a problem! As I write, he is over six feet tall. He will never be sporty but walks to school each day.

Of course, as soon as Matthew could move around, our challenges increased. I did consider tying a bell around his neck to avoid either of us knocking him over, but friends supplied him with loud toys - including a drum (you know who you are, I wasn't grateful at the time), which he loved.

Going out as a family became more difficult at this point. I couldn't push a pram and guide Martyn, so he held onto the pram handles with me. For myself, I couldn't see the ground in front of the pram, as it was too far away, and walked very slowly. We experimented with various types of sling but Matthew didn't like any of them.

As he grew. Matthew adjusted to our limitations. He learned at a young age he needed to make a noise to attract daddy's attention, and as a toddler he would bring toys to us, knowing we would take too long to find the right one ourselves.

Matthew, a Happy, Healthy Toddler

Sharing a sense of humour

He then started to develop a sense of humour. He would creep up on Martyn and then shout. Or he would move his own toothbrush or hairbrush and pretend they were lost, to avoid using them. He knew he didn't need to hide things, in order for us not to find them, he just needed to move them and send us searching.

When Matthew was around three years old, Martyn was watching television one day with the remote control on the arm of his chair. I watched as Matthew crept across to him and moved the controller, replacing it with a toy car from his collection. Matthew and I looked at each other and tried to control our giggles until Martyn put his hand down to change channel and found the car instead. Our little one was testing the boundaries of what we found funny, this was one trick we all appreciated.

Returning to work

When Matthew was six months old, I went back to work. We had very little choice of nursery for him, as there was only one within walking distance of home. Luckily it had a good reputation, and he was very happy there. But I had no-one to share the walk to nursery every day. I would walk him there at 08:00 each day and rush back to fetch him at 18:00, just as they were closing, even though Martyn was home much earlier.

The wilds of the playground again

Applying for a primary school place was also an anxious time. We are lucky to live in an area with several good schools, but again, there is only one within walking distance of home. This is also a good route for Martyn to walk on his own. There was no other school which would suit our needs as parents.

But the rules on school places only consider the needs of the child, not the parents. We were still required to put three school choices on the application form and the wait was an anxious one. Although I had started my business at this point, I did not want to spend hours each day on buses to and from school.

We got our chosen school, and by year two, Martyn and I were sharing the school run. As I said earlier, not long after this Martyn became a governor at the school, and as I write he has held the position of Chair for several years. The walk to the primary school and his bus journey to work are the only routes Martyn can navigate independently. Many parents feel as if they are a taxi service for their children. I spend my time on public transport and walking to ensure both my husband and my son are where they need to be. I don't begrudge this but sometimes it can upset me when I see how easily other people get around in their cars. For a while we were excited at the prospect of driverless cars, but it now seems we would need a driving licence to use them. We are waiting for the day when Matthew can drive.

Probability of inherited sight issues

We knew from the tests before I became pregnant that my visual impairment is unlikely to be passed on, but any child of ours has a 50% chance of developing glaucoma. We have Matthew tested every year and so far, there is no sign of any problem. When he was young, the test had to be carried out under general anaesthetic (echoes of my first contact lens fittings). This is not ideal as it can reduce the pressure in the eye, meaning glaucoma symptoms can be missed. This had happened to Martyn when he was very young. At each appointment I ensured the consultant understood this. I am sure they thought I was a neurotic parent, but Matthew losing his sight reamins one of my greatest fears.

I was very relieved when Matthew was old enough to have the test done while awake. Opticians check for glaucoma with the 'puff of air' test, which might make you blink, but nothing else. Because they need a very accurate measurement of Matthew's eye pressure, they use a probe which touches the eyeball. Matthew has watched his dad have this test several times, and although he doesn't like it, he accepts it will be an annual event for the rest of his life.

At the time of writing, Matthew is in his teens, and with every passing year, it becomes less likely he will develop glaucoma, but my anxiety is still there.

Besides, I want him to be our chauffeur when he reaches driving age!

Matthew

Matthew is very mature for his age, and very empathetic. I believe this is due to him growing up with parents who have particular needs. By the age of eight, he and his dad would go into town on their own, doing a bit of shopping followed by *McDonalds* (well he is our son after all!). Martyn knows his way around Nottingham and can navigate by smell. He always knows when he is passing a *Costa* or a *Subway*.

Matthew has always enjoyed cooking. I will never forget walking into the kitchen when Matthew was about five, to see him and his dad chopping carrots. I took one look at Matthew standing on his step so he could reach the counter top and using a sharp knife, I had to just walk away. I had a similar experience with Matthew using a power drill to drill into a wall under Martyn's direction. I have had to learn trust. Martyn is very careful, and Matthew is very mature. So far, there have been no injuries to either of them.

The Social Model of Disability, and other people's assumptions arose again in the school playground. Matthew would be invited to birthday parties, I would need to find out who was going, and whether they could give him a lift. We live in an affluent area, and the idea of not having a car is strange to a lot of people. Most parents were helpful and would offer a lift, but it was very rare someone would remember and offer without me having to ask. Of course, my parents were always on hand to help, but I wanted my peers in the playground to know our needs and not assume we didn't need any help.

I had the same issues in Matthew's school playground as I had in mine when I was young. I am sure some of the parents thought I was being rude when I didn't notice them or speak to them.

Like any parents, we wanted Matthew to experience as many activities as possible when he was young. With my parents' help, we had taken him to swimming lessons from a very early age. We were relieved he wasn't interested in sport, because his hypermobility would make this difficult, but also because we would never be able to watch him from the touchline.

Music - a passion we can all enjoy

One day when he was seven, Matthew ran excitedly out of school to me.

"Mummy, mummy, there was a man with a trumpet and saxophone and flute at school today. He is coming back next week, and you can come. Will you come mummy? Pleeease..." and on and on all the way home.

The visitor was from Music for Schools, and on his visit the following week he brought with him lots of different woodwind and brass instruments. Matthew blew on a trumpet, and he was immediately hooked. I thought this was because he had been told to blow a raspberry into the trumpet mouthpiece, what seven year old boy doesn't like blowing raspberries? I predicted a short and expensive childhood phase.

I couldn't have been more wrong. Now, Matthew is preparing for Grade 8 trumpet and Grade 6 saxophone. Maybe I should not have complained about the toy drum! He also plays drums (a full-size kit now), guitar and trombone. He is considering a career in music. Once again fate has taken a hand in our lives and given our son a passion we can enjoy despite our limitations. While other parents are out in the cold watching football, we spend our weekends in warm concert halls.

As Matthew grew, my deteriorating reading vision became a problem. I could read easily his early board books and the endless *Biff, Chip and Kipper* books from school, but when he progressed to books with no pictures, I could no longer help him. I needed a magnifying glass to read to him and this was frustrating for both of us.

Also, as a family we can't just jump in a car and go somewhere. Every outing has to be planned and it is hard to be spontaneous.

Our family is a team sport

Martyn and I have always been a good team, now we have a team of three. Martyn and Matthew do all of the cooking (thank goodness) and we have a cleaner. Martyn has started to do the washing too, but sometimes I have to step in to avoid red socks in the white wash. He likes to wear colourful odd socks - and takes pleasure when others point this out, as if he doesn't know it. He will act surprised *"Oh really, I didn't know, I can't see them".*

We have always enjoyed the finer things in life - eating out, cinema, theatre and good wine - and we work hard to afford them. Matthew enjoys this life too, no wine yet though! Hopefully we are inspiring him with our work ethic.

An unusual family life

With two visually impaired people in the house, we have some funny moments. I remember Martyn had put away the shopping one week and when I went to take out my box of tampons, I found a box of OXO cubes instead!

We have always watched a lot of television. In most cases it is our easiest way to see the world, but now Martyn has no sight, I have learned the delights of audio described (AD) programmes. I urge you to try this at least once, as it can be very funny. The audio description has to be fitted between the dialogue, so can sometimes happen before the event it is describing and ruin a scene.

At the cinema some years ago, we were watching *Sherlock Holmes: A Game of Shadows*. Martyn was wearing audio description headphones and I was not. Martyn burst out laughing and it was quite a few seconds before I realised why - a naked Stephen Fry was running across the screen as *Mycroft Holmes*.

The other issue audio describers have is adult content. Often when the AD says, *"they kiss"* I explain to Martyn it is a sex scene. And there is plenty of use of the innuendo. I have heard the term *'banana hammock'* used (look it up for yourself!). The whole family watch *MasterChef* together and we are convinced every sentence of AD in the programme is an innuendo.

The 21st Century is perhaps the best time to be blind, because of the technology. Many household items in our house speak. I remember a cleaner screaming when she accidentally kicked our bathroom scales and they said *"Hello"*. I dare not weigh myself unless I am alone in the house. Martyn has an app on his phone for everything from creating shopping lists, to determining the colour of his clothes.

I am more reticent to take to modern technology and speaking applications. I still live by the mantra of making the most of the useful sight I have, but as my reading vision deteriorates, this may have to change in the future.

Seeing the world

The first holiday Martyn and I had on our own was our honeymoon at Center Parcs, Nottingham, only a 20 minute drive away from home. We had the honeymoon villa with a double jacuzzi - miles away from any of the activities. In our early twenties, we did not have the confidence to travel abroad. At this time, Martyn had as much sight as me, but we chose for the easier option.

Five years later, we had arranged to go on holiday to Tenerife with my parents. This would be our first foreign holiday together, we were both excited and nervous. This was before Martyn lost his sight. A few weeks before the trip, my mum was told she was not allowed to fly for medical reasons. We were devastated but decided to go on our own. I remember the journey to the hotel, giggling in the back of a taxi. We were doing this together and it felt good.

But when we got to the hotel reception, there was a problem. The man behind the desk could not find our reservation. He just kept repeating *"no bordo"* (literally meaning not on board). There was no room for us. When we had cancelled my parents' reservation, the hotel had cancelled ours as well. There was no rep at the hotel in the evening, we did not want to go out into the resort looking for somewhere to stay. Luckily, the manager offered to put us up for one night in a small, dark room usually used by holiday reps.

The next morning, I went down to talk to the rep, who arranged for us to be moved to the room we had paid for. I had been anxious about us travelling alone, but I had not even considered this outcome.

Since then, we have had a holiday every year in the Balearic or the Canary Islands until the Covid-19 pandemic and will continue now the world is getting back to normal.

Blindness and baby made holidays more difficult. There is not a single aspect of air travel I enjoy. Airports are difficult to navigate, with everyone in a hurry and looking out for themselves. The issue starts at check-in. I cannot read the screens at the desks, when we first started to travel

20 years ago, any extra support we could book for the airport started after check-in. So, we would turn up at the special assistance desk and be told to come back when we have checked in.

This has improved dramatically over the years, now we have it down to a fine art, being escorted past the queues at passport control, through to the dreaded scanners.

This part of any journey was made worse for us for a few years when Matthew was small. I dreaded the process of helping Martyn to put his jacket, bag, belt and white cane in a tray to go through the X-ray machine, while carrying Matthew so his buggy could also go through. Then guiding Martyn without his cane and making sure he went through the scanner on his own. All while dodging other people who were trying to do the same. The worst year was when I had a bottle of ready-made milk with me for Matthew and the customs agent insisted, I drink some to prove it was milk.

Of course, this is easier now. Matthew is our chief guide and helper, but we do also book special assistance, so he only has to deal with one of us.

Then there is the air travel itself. On an aeroplane, my eye movement causes extreme dizziness and nausea, which I now know is called positional vertigo. I feel ill for the whole flight every time. I have tried many remedies for this, from traditional travel sickness tablets, to wrist bands, from sedatives to listening to music. Nothing works completely and I sit holding onto the armrests trying to keep my head still as my eyes whirl around. Again, this was most challenging when Matthew was young. I was the only parent who could take him to the toilet on the plane,

She Will Never...

Teamwork at Baggage Claim

which was a nightmare. As he grew older, our solution was for Martyn and Matthew to watch a DVD together while I clung on for dear life to the plane seat - and my breakfast. My vertigo is worst on landing, but luckily goes off within an hour or so of getting off the plane.

Then there is finding the transport to our hotel. We have held up many coaches while we search airport car parks, with me guiding Martyn, and pushing a trolley with our cases on, while searching for a numbered bus.

We always breathe a sigh of relief when we reach our hotel room (checking in at reception is still stressful - we have never forgotten *"no bordo"*).

I can't see myself visiting Australia, or even America, any time soon.

Once we arrive at the resort, it takes us longer than others to find our way around, but then we laze on sunbeds and eat too much, like everyone else.

On the return journey, *'Team Harris'* manage the baggage carousel together. Matthew is chief case-spotter, but until recently didn't have the strength to pull the cases off the belt. It would be my job to place Martyn's hand on the handle, and we would pull together, with me ensuring we did not injure anyone around us in the process.

When Matthew was 12, we went to a resort in Menorca with a high ropes course. Matthew loved it and went on it every day. As I watched him from the ground, I could see the shapes of the obstacles silhouetted against the blue Mediterranean sky. I approached the instructor, *"I am visually impaired"* I told him, *"Can I have a go?"*. The young man looked me up and down and didn't see a white cane or a guide dog, *"Sure,"* he said, *"Grab a harness."*

Five minutes later, I was climbing gingerly up the rickety wooden ladder to the first platform. The first obstacle was a horizontal plank suspended from two ropes. As I stepped onto the plank, it began to swing wildly. I looked down and realised from up here, the wood and rope of the obstacles were completely camouflaged against the brown bark on the ground below. I had lost all contrast and had no useful sight. My brain tried to help, *"Brown"* it said, *"Everything ahead of you is the same shade of brown, you are on level ground, just walk forwards and everything will be fine."* I screamed, much to the embarrassment of my son.

Even when I could see the obstacles, I did not feel confident stretching to reach between the planks and ropes. I pretty much squealed all the way round. Matthew and the instructor gave me directions and support until I completed the course - probably in the slowest time ever. As I descended the rickety ladder to the ground, muttering words to the effect of, *"Flipping heck, never again!"* The onlookers gave me a resounding round of applause, and someone handed me a gin and tonic!

I am not usually so adventurous, and I am not sure what spurred me into this madness. I will not do anything so crazy again.

As we don't have a car, foreign travel is often easier than staying in the UK. However, we have spent time in Scarborough, where our favourite thing to do is to terrify the workers on the Dragon Boats. Their reaction when they see a blind man, a woman who is unsteady on her feet, and a small child getting into a boat together, is hilarious. Remember, Martyn was in the *Sea Scouts* on the Isle of

Man as a boy, and still has his sea legs - we have never had any problem steering round a lake, but the staff don't know that!

A few years ago, we booked to see *Harry Potter and the Cursed Child* in the West End, together with a touch tour of the stage for the whole family. Matthew loved it, he met the actors before the performance and touched the props and learned how the special effects worked. Martyn and I would probably not have booked this just for ourselves but why shouldn't Matthew have some perks out of our disability.

Martyn is more ambitious to see the world than I am. He and Matthew want to visit New York and New Zealand. I am happy to lie on a sun bed and listen to an audiobook.

Treading the boards

Although I had given up my dream of acting for a living, I still longed to be on stage. On every theatre visit, I was imagining being up on the stage, receiving the applause.

In 2015, I had the opportunity to act again. I made a friend who was a member of the local drama group. She invited me to watch her in one of their productions. The group has a purpose built sixty-seater auditorium with professional sound and lighting decks. I insisted on sitting on the front row for the performance. My friend laughed and said I would be very close to the stage. She warned me not to look her in the eye or I would put her off. When I arrived, I found the stage was at the same level as the front row and I was about three feet away from the action. I spent the whole performance watching my friend's feet rather than meeting her eye.

After the first ten minutes, I wanted to be part of this.

My first meeting was a *'read through'* of the next play to be put on. It was *Ten Times Table* by Alan Ayckbourn. The director handed out books of the script. She asked me if I would like to read a part, I jumped at it, but when I saw the size of the text, my heart sank. I was about to hand the book to someone else, when I remembered my new 10x magnifier in my bag. I read the part of Helen, with one eye closed, the book held close to my face. I forgot all embarrassment and enjoyed being included in the group.

The next week was the auditions, I got the part. I was more excited than I had been for many years!

The stage area is small - ideal for me, and I found I could easily learn the lines. Rehearsals were great fun, and I was making new friends. My challenge started at the technical rehearsal - the first time the stage lights were used. At the end of each scene, the stage lights went off, and I would need to get off the stage in the dark. My eyes can take several minutes to adjust, and I was worried I would not be able to safely exit. Of course, this was soon solved. One of the other actors offered to guide me on and off when needed - the audience would never see. It was ironic I was being guided by the actor playing my nemesis in the play!

The cast produce their own costumes, but I am not a seamstress, mentioned in *Chapter One*! One of the cast members made a dress for me out of a pair of curtains. The scene required me to be carried off stage in a fireman's lift (ignoring my positional vertigo for thirty seconds) and crawl back onto stage looking dishevelled. For this reason, the dress had detachable parts so it could look ripped. It was obvious I would not manage the tiny hooks and eyes, and various Velcro fastenings on the dress - so I ended up with a *'dresser'* for the whole run. On one memorable evening he *'pulled the wrong string'* (he is sticking to this story) and as I sat on the stage, the dress gradually slipped down so I was showing far more cleavage than intended!

Since then, I have appeared in several more productions, my experiences have included storming onto stage covered in blood and carrying a wedding dress, playing a Yorkshire matriarch, and a drunken lion! I have overcome my fear of leaving the stage in the dark, and now do this on my own. The tech desk know to give me a bit more time or to leave the 'working lights' on for me.

My biggest personal challenge in the drama group is I don't get as many parts as I would like to. We are a large group with many talented actors. My apologies to anyone who has encountered me after an unsuccessful audition. It is refreshing to be facing the same challenges as my sighted fellow thespians. This is an inclusive group and another example of The Social Model of Disability at work.

As a family, we each have our own interests, and our own strengths. We work well as a team.

How can WE help YOU

As a family we have different perspectives on living with sight loss. We are knowledgeable about organisations and equipment that can help both us and Matthew to enjoy life to the full with our differing abilities. If you have a family member facing sight loss, why not get in touch and tap into our expertise and experience.

Family Team Harris

Epilogue
2020 Vision and Beyond

*Just because a man lacks the use of his eyes,
doesn't mean he lacks vision.*
Stevie Wonder

In common with the rest of the world, my business changed in 2020. Being a Will Writer in a pandemic is *'interesting'*. I produced Wills quickly for those with the virus, I learned to use Zoom, and I overcame the challenges of witnessing Wills while social distancing.

However, my vision for my future had started to change three years earlier...

Professional plans

In 2017, I was given the opportunity to *'tell my story'* at a networking event. The attendees knew me well and I felt confident presenting without notes. For the first time, I told the story of my journey from *'She will never...'* to running my own business. I didn't expect the reaction I received from the room. There was laughter and tears, and more than one member of my audience said I ought to write a book. I dismissed the idea - who would want to read about me?

FAQ

What have you learnt in later life about disability?

Just because I can't do something, doesn't mean I want to do it. Most of my younger years were spent feeling envious of the lives of other people and imagining that they had more fun, more friends, better careers, and generally better lives, than I could ever have. I was often angry and upset.

It took me almost 50 years to fully appreciate that there is more to me than my disability. Yes, I could probably sky dive, but why would I want to? Just because I can't see the ground doesn't make it less deadly if my parachute doesn't open.

I realise that this is a life lesson that many people have to learn the hard way - and I certainly made it hard for myself.

A couple of years later by chance I noticed an advert on social media to write a chapter for a book called *She Can 365*, created by Michelle and Christian Ewen. I was interviewed by Michelle, and by the end of 2019 I was in print! The seed was planted in my brain people may be interested in my story.

Following *She Can 365*, I was invited to tell my story on the *Story Stage* at *Womanifest 2020* in Manchester, to mark International Women's Day. This was a week before the COVID lockdown, I am so glad it went ahead as planned. Again, the response was amazing. The conference was buzzing, I know I am not good in crowds, so I took my support worker. As usual I was confident while presenting on the stage, but I had help to climb down afterwards (black steps with no contrast again!). I began to see a future in professional speaking, but this was not to be in 2020!

Also in 2020, I received a special mention at the Woman Who Achieves Awards. It was the first time I had entered any awards competition and I was overwhelmed. I joined the *Woman Who Academy*, run by *Sandra Garlick MBE* and this amazing group of ladies have helped me to gain the confidence to tell my story. This is also where I met the wonderfully supportive Ladey Adey, my publisher, without whom you would not be reading this book.

I was a finalist at the *Woman Who Awards* and *Today's Wills and Probate Awards* in 2021. I was also a finalist in the *Woman Who Speaks* category in 2022.

I joined the *Professional Speaking Association* in 2021 and entered their Speaker Factor competition. The challenge was to write and perform a five-minute talk - mine was about the high ropes course on holiday.

She Will Never...

Woman Who Achieves Finalist

I won the *East Midlands* heat and went on to the finals. Unfortunately, the performances were on Zoom rather than on stage. Although I didn't win, this was an amazing experience, and I am now part of a supportive community of experienced and expert speakers. My aim is to start a second business working with senior managers to support employees facing challenges.

Family challenges

Although Matthew has been brought up to know our particular needs and to help when he can, we do not expect him to be our full-time carer. We are looking forward to the time that he leaves home in the same way as any other young person, to start his own life. At the time of writing, he has his heart set on Performing Arts College, but we will be proud of him whatever he achieves.

Martyn is enjoying his current role with the Council and now works from home permanently. Martyn and Matthew are discussing visits to New York, Italy and New Zealand. It is ironic that Martyn loves travel more than I do. There is a perception that the blind would not want to see the world. But then Martyn has never conformed to any stereotype.

As for me.... I will never fly an aeroplane, because I choose not to. But also, I will never believe others' perceptions of my abilities and disabilities.

I am the expert on me.

All The Family

Glossary

Word or Phrase	Definition
Education, Health and Care Plan	A legal document that sets out a child or young person's special educational, health and social care needs. It describes the extra help that will be given to meet those needs and how that help will support them to achieve what they want to in their life. https://www.reachingfamilies.org.uk/images/factsheets/education/RF_EHC_PLANS.pdf
Eye Strain (also called Asthenopia)	This refers to a group of symptoms related to the discomfort felt when viewing something, often for prolonged periods. Although often painful, eye strain doesn't lead to permanent eye damage. https://www.specsavers.co.uk/help-and-faqs/what-is-eye-strain-asthenopia

Word or Phrase	Definition
Glaucoma	A common eye condition where the optic nerve, which connects the eye to the brain, becomes damaged. It's usually caused by fluid building up in the front part of the eye, which increases pressure inside the eye. Glaucoma can lead to loss of vision if it is not diagnosed and treated early. https://www.nhs.uk/conditions/glaucoma/
Joint Hypermobility Syndrome	Very flexible joints and it causes you pain (you may think of yourself as double jointed). It usually affects children and young people and often gets better as you get older. https://www.nhs.uk/conditions/joint-hypermobility-syndrome/
Nystagmus	A condition of uncontrolled eye movement. If you have nystagmus your eyes move or "wobble" constantly. This can be in a side to side, an up and down or a circular motion or a combination of these. This uncontrolled movement can affect how clearly you can see. https://www.rnib.org.uk/sites/default/files/Nystagmus-2020.pdf
Optic Nerve Atrophy, also known as Congenital Optic Nerve Atrophy or Optic Neuropathy.	The optic nerve is composed of nerve fibres that transmit impulses to the brain. In the case of optic atrophy, something is interfering with the optic nerve's ability to transmit these impulses. https://my.clevelandclinic.org/health/diseases/12326-optic-atrophy

Glossary

Word or Phrase	Definition
Polycystic Ovary Syndrome	A common condition which affects how a woman's ovaries work. It causes irregular periods (or no periods at all) and difficulty getting pregnant due to irregular ovulation, or no ovulation at all. The condition is very common, and is thought to affect around one in every ten women in the UK. https://www.nhs.uk/conditions/polycystic-ovary-syndrome-pcos/
Positional Vertigo or Benign Paroxysmal Positional Vertigo	A common cause of dizziness. It occurs in people of all ages, but is more common in middle aged or elderly people. It causes short bursts of intense dizziness when the body or head is placed in certain positions such as lying on one side in bed or looking upwards. People can feel sick and sometimes unsteady for a few hours after the dizziness has gone away. https://www.nhs.uk/conditions/vertigo/
Purpura also called Blood Spots or Skin Haemorrhages	Refers to purple-colored spots on the skin. The spots may also appear on organs or mucous membranes, including the inside of the mouth. Purpura occurs when small blood vessels burst, causing blood to pool under the skin. This can create purple spots on the skin from small dots to large patches. Purpura spots are generally benign, but may indicate a more serious medical condition. https://www.healthline.com/health/purpura

Word or Phrase	Definition
Squint also called Strabismus	This is where the eyes point in different directions. It is particularly common in young children, but can occur at any age. One of the eyes may turn in, out, up or down while the other eye looks ahead. https://www.nhs.uk/conditions/squint/
Statement of Special Educational Needs	This sets out your child's needs and the help they should have. It is issued by your Local Education Authority. This has now been replaced by the Education, Health and Care (EHC) Plan.
Trabeculectomy	This is an operation which helps to drain fluid out of the eye and into a small blister (called a bleb) under the surface of the eye (the conjunctiva). The operation creates a kind of trap door for the fluid to pass through, bypassing the normal drainage channel. Drainage of aqueous is improved and this reduces intraocular pressure. https://glaucoma.uk/about-glaucoma/treatments-surgery/trabeculectomy-surgery/

References

Books

Ayckbourn, Alan, *Ten Times Table*, (Samuel French), 2015

Bond, Michael, *A Bear Called Paddington*, (Harper Collins Children's Books), 1958

Eddings, David and Eddings, Leigh, *The Belgariad*, (Del Rey Books), 1982-1994

Edwards, Dorothy, *My Naughty Little Sister*, Young Puffin Books, 1973

Ewen, Michelle and Ewen, Christian, *She Can 365*, (Team Author UK), 2020

Grahame, Kenneth, *The Wind in the Willows*, (Methuen), 1908

Norton, Mary, *The Borrowers*, (Dent), 1962

Shakespeare, William, MacBeth, (Penguin Classics), 1987

Films

Sherlock Holmes: A Game of Shadows, Crime, Guy Ritchie, (Warner Brothers Pictures), London, 2011

The Rescuers, Children's, Wolfgang Reitherman, John Lounsbery, Art Stevens, (Walt Disney Productions), 1977

Working Girl, Romantic Comedy, Mike Nichols, (20th Century Fox), New York, 1988

Music

Meat Loaf, *Two Out of Three Ain't Bad*, Epic, 1978, CD, 1978, Bat Out of Hell

The Everly Brothers, *All I have to do is Dream*, Cadence, 1948, 1958, CD, 1958, The Very Best of the Everly Brothers

Wham!, *Last Christmas*, Columbia- Epic- CBS, 1984, CD, 1984, Last Christmas

Whitney Houston, *Saving all my Love for You*, Avista, 1985, CD, 1985, Whitney Houston

Pictures

Mona Lisa, *Leonardo da Vinci*, (The Louvre Museum, Paris), since 1804

Photographs

All photographs are family pictures with the exception of: *About the Author* and *Back Cover* by Gemma Wilks of Stand Out Get Noticed Ltd.

Photograph of *Haylee* using the Perkins Brailler courtesy of L. Penny Rosenblum, PhD https://www.pathstoliteracy.org.

Television (TV) Programmes

Charlie's Angels, *Aaaron Spelling and Leonard Goldberg*, (Columbia Pictures Television) 1976-1981

The Last Leg, *Andrew Beint and Danny Carr,* (Channel Four) from 2012

Theatre

Harry Potter and the Cursed Child, *Jack Thorne, JK Rowling, Tom Tiffany,* Palace Theatre, London. Opened 2016.

The Phantom of the Opera, *Andrew Lloyd Webber*, lyrics by *Charles Hart*, and a libretto by *Lloyd Webber and Richard Stilgoe,* His Majesty's Theatre, London. Opened 1986

Websites

1957 Flu Epidemic, https://www.britannica.com/event/1957-flu-pandemic, 01/09/2022

Benign Paroxsymal Positional Vertigo (BPPV), University Hospital Southampton, NHS, Benign paroxysmal positional vertigo - patient information https://www.nhs.uk/conditions/vertigo, 24/05/2021

References

Glaucoma Treatments https://glaucoma.uk/about-glaucoma/treatments-surgery/trabeculectomy-surgery, 06/10/2021

Gov.uk, Reasonable adjustments: a legal duty - GOV.UK https://www.gov.uk/government/publications/reasonable-adjustments-a-legal-duty/reasonable-adjustments-a-legal-duty, 07/10/2021

Guide Dogs UK, Charity for the Blind and Partially Sighted, https://www.guidedogs.org.uk, 12/10/2021

Joint Hypermobility Syndrome - NHS https://www.nhs.uk/conditions/joint-hypermobility-syndrome, 15/10/2021

Nationwide Children's, Immune Thrombocytopenic Purpura in Children https://www.nationwidechildrens.org/conditions/health-library/immune-thrombocytopenic-purpura-in-children, 06/10/2021

Paths to Literacy, Penny Rosenblum, https://www.pathstoliteracy.org/dots-families-introduction-braille-writing, 18/08/2022

Polycystic Ovary Syndrome, NHS https://www.nhs.uk/conditions/polycystic-ovary-syndrome-pcos, 21/11/2021

Reaching Families, RF EHC PLANS https://www.reachingfamilies.org.uk/images/factsheets/education/RF_EHC_PLANS.pdf, 15/11/2021

RNIB, Registering as sight impaired - RNIB - See differently, https://www.rnib.org.uk/eye-health/registering-your-sight-loss, 04/10/2021

Specsavers, What is eye strain/asthenopia? Specsavers UK, https://www.specsavers.co.uk/help-and-faqs/what-is-eye-strain-asthenopia, 07/10/2021

Some Famous Nystagmus Sufferers

You may be interested to know famous nystagmus sufferers include author and presenter *Richard Osman*, who supports the Nystagmus Network®, and the flautist *Sir James Galway* OBE. Former MP *David Blunkett's* blindness was caused by improperly developed optic nerves due to a rare genetic disorder.

The world worries about disability more than disabled people do.
Warwick Davis

Acknowledgements

Family

Martyn Harris	My husband and best friend - for keeping the household tasks going while I was writing.
Matthew Harris	My son - for his support and living with the embarrassment of having me as his mum.
Brenda Bell	My mum - for her support and love, insights into my early life, and constant red pen.
David Bell	My wonderful dad, - who is battling dementia, who may never read this book and find out how much I love and respect him.

Organisations

Vivien Jones	Nystagmus Network® - for her amazing Preface.
Sue Ricketts	Nystagmus Network® - for her continuous support and constructive criticism as a Beta Reader.

Book Production

Beta Readers	**Sue Ricketts, Sandra Garlick MBE, Tracey Tongue Stuckey, Jackie Monk, Penny Lewin and Dawn Owen** - for their encouragement, and constructive comments.

She Will Never...

Andy Bounds   For his continued support and such a powerful Foreword

Chris Ryder   For her wonderful cartoon illustrations and her patience with me.

and last but not least!

Ladey Adey   Without her confidence in me, there would not have been a book.

Amanda Harris - Author

About the Author
Amanda Harris

Amanda grew up in Doncaster, South Yorkshire. She is an only child and attended Wakefield Girls' High School before Worcester College for the Blind and studying Law at Nottingham Trent University. She has been visually impaired since birth.

Amanda has run a successful business as a Will Writer since 2011. She is married to Martyn, who is blind, and they have one son, Matthew. They live in Nottingham. She has a love for theatre and amateur dramatics in which she is an active member of West Bridgford Dramatic Society. She also enjoys eating out, music and history.

Contact Me:

Website: www.amandaharris.co.uk

LinkedIn: linkedin.com/in/amanda-harris-138a2699

email: hello@amandaharris.co.uk

How can I help YOU?

Amanda - Speaker

I deliver:

Keynote Motivational Presentations.

Interactive workshops and training.

Humorous talks about disability.

To:

Small and medium sized businesses.

Primary schools.

Secondary schools within the PSHE curriculum.

Small local groups.

My topics include:

Equality, diversity and inclusion.

Overcoming challenges.

Communication within teams.

How to book me:

Just ask.

This list of topics I speak and train on is not exhaustive and not all of my work is around visual impairment. Remember, a small change can make a huge difference.

If you would like more information

- again just ask!

Index

She Will Never...

Team Harris

Your Notes

A few pages for you to make your own notes.

She Will Never...

Your Notes

She Will Never...

Endorsements

Amanda Harris' *She Will Never...* is one of those books that you start and simply can't put down. Despite visual impairment from birth, Amanda hasn't let her disability define her, but has found a way to inspire others by sharing her story demonstrating her determination, perseverance, and humour. This book clearly shows the reader that no matter what barriers you face in life, there is always a way to achieve something. I strongly encourage you to grab a copy, and then book Amanda to speak at your event. She will wow your audience.

Sandra Garlick MBE,
Founder of Woman Who

She will never... is the book the nystagmus community has been waiting for. No one has shared the highs and lows of living with this complex eye condition with quite so much humour, openness, resonance or self-deprecation. We simply can't wait to read it, to get to know Amanda and immerse ourselves in her nystagmus experience.

Nystagmus is notoriously difficult to explain, partly because it's different for everyone, but Amanda's engaging writing style draws us in and invites us to see the world in sharp focus through her eyes.

For many, like Amanda, being told you will never achieve something can be just the catalyst you need to win at life.

Sue Ricketts,
Nystagmus Network®

She Will Never...